HAMMER, OAK, AND LIGHTNING:

A Thor Devotional

Thor, or Donner, as envisioned by Arthur Rackham in his illustrations of
Wagner's *Ring of the Nibelung* cycle of operas.

HAMMER, OAK, AND LIGHTNING:

A Thor Devotional

by Jeremy Baer

The Troth
2019

Published by The Troth
325 Chestnut Street, Suite 800
Philadelphia, PA 19106
http://www.thetroth.org/

ISBN-13: 978-1-941136-27-0 (hardcover)
978-1-941136-28-7 (paperback)
978-1-941136-29-4 (e-book)

Cover design: Ben Waggoner
Cover photo: Mélody P, on Unsplash.com (https://unsplash.com/@melodyp)
Troth logo designed by Kveldúlfr Gundarsson, drawn by 13 Labs, Chicago, Illinois

I dedicate this book to Freyja.
While one of my oathholders, she has many others
who can speak on her behalf.
She graciously "loaned" out my time and talents
to give a much needed voice to her compatriot,
the thundering son of Odin.

Thor defeating Thrym and his horde of giants, as envisioned by the Danish artist Louis Moe (1898). Courtesy of the Dansk Skolemuseum. Wikimedia Commons CC BY-SA 4.0.

CONTENTS

Author's Foreword

Þórr. Thor, the son of Odin. He is strongest of the gods and wielder of Mjolnir. "Thunderer," some call him, and "Red Beard," too.

Germanic polytheism is commonly referred to as Heathenry, and its devotees commonly call themselves Heathens. As far as the evidence can tell, Thor has been a major deity throughout all epochs of Heathenry. In the Viking Age he was unarguably the most popular god, at least in Iceland. Today among Heathens he enjoys a sizable following.

I first encountered Thor in the stories in the *Prose Edda* and *Poetic Edda*. It seemed to me that the lore of those two works was largely the adventures of Odin, Thor and Loki, with the other deities appearing sporadically. Thor's strength and no-nonsense approach to life immediately appealed to me. The All-Father has magic and wisdom, but if you want a god to play the heavy in a fight, you call on Thor.

My first exposure to Thor from a specifically modern polytheist perspective was found in Volume One of *Our Troth*. This was written by various authors from The Troth, the inclusive Heathen organization of which I am a member and on whose board of directors I currently serve. The section on Thor, like the rest of that volume, is a well-crafted article from a variety of perspectives.

Why, then, should I write a book on Thor? The impetus did not originate as a vague creative impulse, but rather as a strong request. Within my private esoteric excursions, it was opined that Odin, Freya and even Loki all enjoy a sizeable following within various polytheist communities. Odin especially has a large cache of writers and occultists who have written books about him, composed poetry to him, and performed various types of magic in his name. But what of Odin's most famous son, the mighty Thor? What does he have?

I performed a search for "Thor" on Amazon. I was of course inundated by results from the comic book Thor of *Marvel* fame. For the record, I am **not** a fan of that genre. Filtering those results out, I was able to find Thor (or some version of him) as the subject of various fantasy novels and young adult books. But of specifically pagan or Heathen devotional books there seemed few to none, at least within the last few years.

It was suggested I do something to address the issue. Even though my oaths lay to Odin and Freyja, I have always respected Thor greatly. When given the task I gave no objection. I feel I owe the deity a certain recompense for the protection he has given me. "A gift for a gift," as we like to say in Heathenry.

My hope is that here I have furnished a devotional dedicated solely to Thor, the son of Odin. And when I say "dedicated," I mean it in the true sense of the word—a labor of sincerity and love, from a loyal follower in service to one of his deities.

In the interests of providing a thorough and workable devotional work to Thor, I have tried to attack the problem from a variety of perspectives: academic, personal and liturgical. However, different aspects of this book may appeal to different types. For instance, there are some Heathens who may not appreciate my UPG (*unverified personal gnosis*—personal insights that are not derived from the ancient written sources). Others may find the minutiae of Lore rather boring. Others may find that some of the rites or meditations I propose do not resonate with them. Certainly, this book is not meant for those looking for a purely academic overview of Thor. Nor is it written for those wanting another treatment of the comic book version of Thor.

If someone doesn't like something written herein, so be it. Reasonable people can disagree. I invite them to write their own book. I am but one voice, and I welcome other voices at the table. The only voices I don't entreat are those who would misuse the name of Thor or any of the other gods of Heathenry in service of racialism. To them I have nothing to say. This book is *not* written for them, and their opinion is not solicited.

I hope my work adds to the Heathen and polytheist communities, and does justice to the god of whom I write. Hail Thor!

—Jeremy J. Baer
March 2019

Thor as envisioned by the Swedish sculptor Bengt Erland Fogelberg, 1842.
Photo from Guerber, *Myths of the Norsemen.*

PART I: LORE

Knowledge of, and respect for, ancient texts varies widely among individuals and groups within Heathenry and paganism. At one end, I have seen groups of highly erudite people who are blessed with a supreme command of the most arcane details. One can respect their knowledge, though at times some of these individuals seem to treat polytheism as a book club, rather than a spiritual faith. At the other end are people who eschew crusty old texts written in another time and place, dismissing such information as outdated for the modern age. The problem is that the personal gnosis they seek, untethered to any proper historical grounding, sometimes takes them well beyond what most of us can comfortably recognize as the boundaries of our traditions.

Most of the individuals reading this work probably tread somewhere in the middle ground, not disdainful of the ancient texts, though perhaps not having the ability or inclination to study them in their deepest levels. I present this Lore overview for their benefit, designed to acquaint the reader with the most crucial texts on Thor and the highlights of what is said therein.

How Thor is broadly viewed within the Lore will help the reader identify, in Part Two, how and why he was historically honored. The Lore notes in Part One also underpin many of my personal observations and rituals discussed in Part Three.

How Thor was seen in a former era may not necessarily be the end of the story for us moderns, but it is undeniably the beginning. In other words, history and tradition may not be the only elements used in constructing a working edifice for honoring Thor, but they are the critical foundations on which everything else rests.

Chapter One: The Prose Edda

The *Prose Edda* is assumed to be the work of Snorri Sturluson.

Snorri lived from about 1178 to 1241 CE. From early childhood to his assassination, Snorri's life story was forged by medieval Icelandic politics. In order to mitigate a feud, he was fostered by a man who was of higher social station than his own father. Snorri received a learned upbringing and was later married off to a wealthy woman. He served twice as Lawspeaker, Iceland's nominal head-of-state. He became entangled in the politics of the Norwegian throne and the latter's desire to extend influence in Iceland. Ultimately, Snorri was murdered by agents recruited by the King of Norway, the price of his political ambitions (Sturluson, pp. xii-xiii).

Snorri (or whoever wrote the *Prose Edda*) seemed conversant with classical mythology and poetry. The author's chief purpose in writing the work was to preserve the mythopoetic heritage of Iceland, and to explain to poets some of the complicated mythological allusions inherent in skaldic poetry. The original manuscript of the *Prose Edda* written in the thirteenth century doesn't survive, but later copies do. By later medieval times it was considered the authoritative manual to teach traditional verse forms (Sturluson, *Edda*, pp. xi-xii).

The *Prose Edda's* accuracy is sometimes suspect. It was composed some two centuries after Iceland's conversion. There is a question of whether Snorri truly understood the myths he was describing. Did he unconsciously frame the myths into a false narrative inspired by his classical education and knowledge of Latin poetics? Did he deliberately censor or edit Heathen myths that did not agree with his Christian upbringing? Did he confabulate myths wholesale, if it served his poetic sensibilities? (Tolley, p. 21) The *Prose Edda* often references the *Poetic Edda,* and where it does Snorri probably stands on the surest footing. In other areas, Snorri's version of events differs from existing lore. The most egregious example is the tale he tells of Balder and Loki, which radically departs from the version given by a Danish author, Saxo Grammaticus (Saxo, pp. 69-76). The figures of a Christ-like Balder and a Devil-like Loki are sometimes taken as the best evidence of Snorri's alleged Christian interpolation.

At the end of the day, the *Prose Edda* stands second only to the *Poetic Edda* as a repository of Lore, but it must be taken into critical context.

The *Prose Edda* is divided into the following parts, wherein I will summarize Thor's exploits.

Prologue

Snorri was influenced by a Christian upbringing as well as an education that referenced the classical literary heritage. This would be true in general of the intelligentsia of his day, the literary elite for whom he was writing. For the Norse myths to be palatable to a contemporary audience, they had to somehow fit within that Christian and classical spectrum.

The prologue of the *Prose Edda* begins with the Biblical account of Noah and the Flood (Sturluson, *Edda*, p. 3). It then proceeds to Troy, the legendary city whose famous war served to underpin Greco-Roman myth. Thor is euhemerized as a human prince of Troy, one of exceptional physical strength (Sturluson, *Edda*, pp. 5-6). After killing many humans and monsters and beasts, Thor takes over the land of Thrace, likened here to Thrudheim. He marries a Sibyl, a prophetess, named Sif. They have many sons. Eventually Odin is born into the mix, and Odin goes on to settle north and sire the other characters of Norse myth (Sturluson, *Edda*, pp. 6-7).

When Roman poets needed an origin story, they invented the tale that they were founded by Aeneas, a Trojan prince who escaped the fires of Troy. (Romulus and Remus, the twins who ultimately founded Rome, were descended from Aeneas.) That several centuries separated the sack of Troy from the founding of Rome didn't matter, so long as Roman history was firmly embedded in the prestigious world of Greek myth. Snorri takes a page from them and tethers Norse myth to the same world of Greek myth, while also being careful to wink at the Christian Genesis story. This is perhaps not terribly surprising for a man of his day. What is curious is the reversing of the parental dynamics between Thor and Odin.

The Deluding of Gylfi

Gylfaginning (The Deluding of Gylfi) concerns a sorcerer-king, Gylfi, who tries to infiltrate the world of the gods. He encounters three beings who are considered avatars of Odin. They relay the scope of the mythological world to him, from creation to the rebirth of the world after Ragnarok (Sturluson, *Edda*, pp. 9-10).

Below I have tried to separate mentions of Thor into logical chunks.

In The Beginning

The world came about because fire and ice met in a great void. The union of these polarities gave birth to various primordial beings. Odin and his two brothers murdered Ymir, a primordial entity, and from Ymir's various anatomical parts and detritus Odin fashioned the world. Odin and his two brothers then went on to create humanity from the driftwood of ash and elm trees (Sturluson, *Edda*, pp. 12-18).

Earth was in some sense Odin's creation, a daughter, and a goddess in her own right. Odin coupled with her, and the union brought forth his eldest and most famous son, Thor. Thor is formally referred to as Ása-Thor: Thor of the *Æsir*, the tribe of deities to which Odin and Thor belong (Sturluson, *Edda*, p. 18). Thor is also called Öku-Thor, the charioteer, for he owns a chariot drawn by two male goats, Tanngnjóstr and Tanngrisnir (Tooth Gnasher and Snarl Tooth) (Sturluson, *Edda*, p. 32).

He rules over a realm called Thrudvang (*Þrúðvangr*, Plains of Strength) in a hall called Bilskirnir, which is alleged to be the largest hall ever built. (As god of the common man, Thor has many followers and thus needs large facilities to accommodate them.) Thor's three prized possessions are the hammer Mjolnir, the iron gloves he uses to grip the hammer, and his belt of strength (*megingjörð*) which doubles his might when worn (Sturluson, *Edda*, p. 32).

Thor and the Master Builder

The gods had wrought Midgard, the realm of humanity, and they had built Valhalla, Odin's magnificent hall of the slain. But they were not yet themselves secure in lodgings, and this presented a danger because troublesome giants infested the lands (Sturluson, *Edda*, p. 50). What to do?

Almost on cue, a mysterious smith arrived to court the gods. He promised to build an impregnable fortress in three seasons. As payment he asked for the sun and moon—and also for the hand of the beautiful Freyja. The

Thor as sculpted by Carl Johan Bonnesen, on the roof of the
Ny Carlsberg Bryghus, Copenhagen, Denmark. Photo by Matthew Black,
Wikimedia Commons. CC BY-SA 2.0.

gods bartered, saying they would agree to his terms if he completed the edifice in one season, as opposed to three, and any part left unfinished meant
the contract had not been fulfilled (Sturluson, *Edda*, pp. 50-51).

The gods did not expect the smith to complete the work in time, which
is why they had agreed to the bargain. But with the help of his horse, Svadil-
fari, the mysterious smith had nearly completed the fortress by the dead-
line. In a panic, the gods decided that Loki bore the brunt of criticism for
making this unwise compact, and thus it was his problem to fix. Loki's
shapeshifting and gender-bending solution was to disguise himself as a mare
to "distract" the smith's stallion. From this union ultimately came Odin's
eight-legged steed, Sleipnir, the best horse in the Nine Worlds (Sturluson,
Edda, pp. 51-52).

The stratagem worked. The smith fell behind schedule. In his subse-
quent rage, the smith revealed himself as a giant. He had nearly gained the
heavens and the hand of Freyja by luring the gods into what had seemed
to them a fool's bargain. But with his guise foiled, the gods simply recalled
Thor. He had been away in the east fighting giants, but came promptly

5

when summoned. His hammer soon found its way into the unnamed giant's skull, shattering it into several pieces (Sturluson, *Edda*, p. 52).

Presumably the gods finished the last bit of construction and had themselves a first-rate fortress. We are sadly not told what Thor's reaction was to a pregnant Loki.

That Really Got His Goat!

Thor and Loki seem to have been traveling companions before the death of Balder.

On one such adventure, Thor and Loki happened to stay at a farm. Thor's goats not only pulled his chariot, but they provided him endless food. They could be cooked and then returned to life the next day, provided their bones were left intact and were subsequently consecrated by the hammer Mjolnir (Sturluson, *Edda*, pp. 53-54).

Unfortunately, the farmer's children, Thjalfi and Roskva, were not aware of this. Thjalfi sucked the marrow out of one of the goat's thighbones. When it came back to life the next day, it was lame in one leg. Thor was furious (Sturluson, *Edda*, p. 54). Thor could have taken the simple precaution of warning the boy not to touch the goat's legs. Presumably, though, it was unspoken wisdom that one does not touch property belonging to a guest, especially if the guest was a god.

The farmer was terrified of Thor's rage and offered him everything. Thor, to his credit, quickly calmed down. He took Thjalfi and Roskva as his bond servants in compensation (Sturluson, *Edda*, p. 54), and the boy would later serve as Thor's second in a duel against the giant Hrungnir.

One Glove Fits All

Thor left the goats behind. He, Loki, and his new bond servants continued their travels.

Food was running low. They came across an enormous hall where they took shelter. An earthquake in the middle of the night startled them. Thor went to investigate and heard a roaring noise. At sunrise, the source of the noise became apparent in the form of a large man, snoring as he slumbered (Sturluson, *Edda*, p. 55).

Thor's natural instinct was of course to smash the stranger's skull with his hammer. However, the stranger awoke to a startled Thor and introduced himself as Skrymir. Skrymir knew exactly who Thor was, and the stranger asked about his glove. Thor realized the hall he taken shelter in was, in fact, a giant glove (Sturluson, *Edda*, p. 55).

Thor encountering Skrymir, as envisioned by the artist Louis Huard.
Keary and Keary, *The Heroes of Asgard* (1871).

Third Time Not the Charm

Skrymir offered to join them on their journey; Thor accepted, presumably to ascertain his identity. They pooled food supplies and stored them in Skrymir's bag. Skrymir fell asleep under the oak tree. Thor went to untie the food bag. He found, amazingly, that his strength failed him and he could not untie it (Sturluson, *Edda*, p. 56).

Realizing that he had been duped twice, and that the mysterious stranger seemed to be the cause of it, Thor resolved to end things with his usual customary efficiency— a hammer to the head. Three times, throughout the night, he tried to smash Skrymir's skull. But the stranger was seemingly unharmed and laughed off each attempt as (respectively) leaves, acorns and birds (Sturluson, *Edda*, pp. 56-57).

The Trials of the Companions

Skrymir awoke the next day to say the stronghold known at Utgard lay ahead, and they could find hospitality under its lord, Utgarda-Loki. He cautioned a humbled Thor not to brag in the lord's presence. With that, Skrymir disappeared (Sturluson, *Edda*, p. 57).

Thor and his companions entered the massive fortress known as Utgard, populated by rather large men. They were welcomed by the lord, Utgarda-Loki. Whenever deities enter a giant's hall, they are usually subjected to some manner of contest, mental or physical. True to form, Utgarda-Loki proposed contests for the guests to test their mettle (Sturluson, *Edda*, pp. 57-58).

Loki Laufeyson boasted he could devour food faster than anyone else. But when the lord of the keep pitted Loki against a fellow named Logi, Laufeyson lost the speed-eating contest (Sturluson, *Edda*, p. 58).

Thjalfi, meanwhile, said he was a fast runner. He was matched in a foot race against a fellow named Hugi, and lost three times in a row (Sturluson, *Edda*, p. 58). As for Roskva, we are not told if she participated. Possibly, as a female, she was not subject to the same manly feats of strength expected of the males.

The Trials of Thor

If Loki was an eater, Thor was a drinker. The son of Odin asked to see if he could chug down some alcohol faster than anyone. Utgarda-Loki brought the hall's ceremonial horn, and bid Thor drink of it. Three times he tried to empty the vessel, but despite quaffing down an enormous amount Thor could not drain it (Sturluson, *Edda*, p. 60).

Having failed at this, Thor was subjected to a wrestling contest. Utgarda-Loki pitted Thor first against his cat, and then against an old female nurse called Elli. Thor could not manage more than to lift the cat's paw. Against Elli he held out for a while but ultimately was thrown to the ground (Sturluson, *Edda*, pp. 60-61).

But They Were All of Them Deceived

The next morning Thor and his companions were graciously treated to a fine breakfast, after which Utgarda-Loki escorted them outside. As they were about to leave, Thor bemoaned his poor standing in the contests, worrying for his reputation. Utgarda-Loki then revealed himself and Skrymir as the same individual, a shape-shifting giant capable of great illusions (Sturluson, *Edda*, p. 61).

Skrymir's food bag had been secured with an iron wire, which is why Thor couldn't untie it. Meanwhile, Thor's three hammer blows to Skrymir's skull had instead struck a flat-topped mountain, and the hammer blows had caused great square-shaped valleys to appear (Sturluson, *Edda*, p. 62). Loki had lost the eating contest because Logi was wildfire incarnate. Likewise, Thjalfi could not win a footrace against Hugi, who was thought itself (Sturluson, *Edda*, p. 62).

Thor's drinking contest had been against the ocean, and he lowered it to such a degree that it had caused the tides. The "cat" he had wrestled had been Thor's great nemesis, the Midgard Serpent, whose coils entangled the earth. Thor had lifted the serpent nearly to the sky. The old nurse Elli was in reality Old Age incarnate, and Thor lasted longer against her than anyone else (Sturluson, *Edda*, p. 62).

The giant confessed to being overawed by Thor's power and suggested that should they ever meet again, the giant's only defense would be more trickery. With that, Utgard and Utgarda-Loki vanished, much to Thor's chagrin, as he was quite in the mood to smash something with his hammer (Sturluson, *Edda*, p. 63).

Gone Fishing

Thor, still bristling from his encounters with Utgarda-Loki, decided to test his mettle in another adventure. This time it was Thor who used illusions: he disguised himself as a young boy. Companionless, he set out to find the Midgard Serpent (Sturluson, *Edda*, p. 63).

He came across the giant Hymir and the two agreed to go fishing, but Hymir was dubious that this "young boy" could offer much help. The two did not get along, but Thor refrained from using his hammer because he had bigger fish to catch (quite literally). When the subject of bait was broached, Thor ripped off the head of the largest ox around (Sturluson, *Edda*, pp. 63-64).

Thor kept demanding the two row further out to sea, but Hymir was increasingly nervous that they had left safety behind and were in the realm of the Midgard Serpent. When they had gone far enough, he baited the hook with the ox head and lowered it deep into the waters. The creature took the bait, and suddenly Thor and the Midgard Serpent were locked in a contest of strength. Thor fell through the boat and was now bracing himself against the sea floor, trying to bring the serpent to heel (Sturluson, *Edda*, p. 64).

Hymir realized he had been duped. He became quite terrified of the struggle (even giants fear the Midgard Serpent). He cut Thor's line and the Midgard Serpent fell back into the waters. Thor threw his hammer after the creature, but yet it lived, waiting for a rematch at Ragnarok. A punch from Thor sent Hymir into the ocean, and a frustrated son of Odin waded back to the shore (Sturluson, *Edda*, pp. 64-65).

The Altuna stone from Uppland, Sweden, showing Thor fishing for the Midgard Serpent. Note that his foot has gone through the bottom of the boat. Uppland, Sweden. Image by Gunnar Creutz, Wikimedia Commons. CC SA 3.0.

Hallowing the Fire

At some point, at least as Snorri tells the tale, Loki changed from the bumbling trickster-like associate of the gods to a *bona fide* miscreant and menace. Loki arranged the death of Balder, Odin's son who was beloved by the gods (Sturluson, *Edda*, pp. 65-66).

10

At Balder's funeral pyre, Thor raised Mjolnir to hallow the fire. When a dwarf named Lit got in his way, Thor kicked him. The hapless creature landed to its fiery death within the pyre (Sturluson, *Edda*, p. 67). Casual mean-spiritedness or meaningful sacrifice?

Ragnarok

The gods are fated to fight the fire giants of Muspelheim and the frost giants in a cataclysmic event known as Ragnarok. Odin leads the gods and his honor guard of the slain, the *Einherjar*, to battle. As Snorri tells the tale, Loki and his offspring ally with the giants. In this battle, Odin, Freyr and Tyr are killed (Sturluson, *Edda*, pp. 71-73). Thor himself also dies. Thor encounters the Midgard Serpent once more. He cannot save his father, Odin, from death because he is occupied with the serpent. Thor kills the serpent with his hammer, but not before the serpent sprays Thor with poison, to which Thor soon succumbs (Sturluson, *Edda*, p. 73).

The world is reborn after the fires of Ragnarok. The sons of Thor, Modi and Magni, are present. They carry with them their slain father's hammer Mjolnir (Sturluson, *Edda*, p. 77).

Poetic Diction

Skáldskaparmál (Poetic Diction) provides mythological background to many of the cryptic references and stock phrases that were used in skaldic poetry. A magician named Ægir or Hlér journeys to the gods and feasts with them. He is seated next to Bragi, either a son of Odin or a man deified because of his poetry. Bragi relays many mythological stories to Ægir. Thor is listed in the retinue of gods and goddesses that receive Ægir (Sturluson, *Edda*, pp. 80-81). Below are the sections that pertain to Thor.

Study for a statue of Thor killing the Midgard Serpent, by Swedish sculptor Bengt Erland Fogelberg. National Museum of Fine Arts, Stockholm. CC PD 1.0.

The Fight with Hrungnir

One can read this tale two ways. Either Odin's reckless actions lead to a mess that Thor must clean up. Or (more likely) it is a stratagem to lure a giant away from his home base and have Thor assassinate him. If the latter was the All-Father's plan, however, it did not seem to be disclosed beforehand to Thor.

Odin conspicuously rides his horse Sleipnir into the realm of giants and deliberately extols his steed at the expense of Hrungnir's steed, Gullfaxi (Golden Mane). Incensed, the giant chases Odin all the way into Asgard. Once in Asgard everyone makes a pretense of the niceties that define guest-host relationship. Hrungnir demands food and drink and is provided such, though after some alcohol he makes a point to repay Odin with some obnoxious boasting of his own (Sturluson, *Edda*, pp. 86-87).

The gods ask Thor to provide a heavy presence to deter Hrungnir's boastings. Thor's immediate reaction is to suggest violence. Hrungnir, however, points out that he is both a guest and weaponless—there is no honor to be had if Thor slays him. He proposes a better test of strength and courage by challenging Thor to a duel at the border between Asgard and Giant-Land (Sturluson, *Edda*, p. 87). The time came for the duel. It seems the custom for duels is that each participant is to have an assistant. Thor brought Thjalfi, his human servant. The giants, meanwhile, created a monstrous golem-like creature out of clay, and imbued it with the heart of a mare. It was called Mökkurkalfi (Mist-Calf). This creature, despite his monstrous size, wet himself in fear at the sight of Thor. Thjalfi attacked Mökkurkalfi; the latter, we are told, fell without much of a fight (Sturluson, *Edda*, p. 88). Meanwhile, Hrungnir and Thor spied each other from a distance and threw their respective weapons, a whetstone and the hammer, at each other. The weapons collided in midair; part of the whetstone crashed to earth, whence all other whetstones are derived, and the other part lodged itself in Thor's head. The hammer, however, struck Hrungnir in his stone head, killing him (Hollander, p. 88).

Thor intended to gift Hrungnir's steed, Gullfaxi, to his infant child, Magni. Odin objected, saying Magni was the offspring of the giantess Járnsaxa, and that the father of the gods was a more deserving recipient than the boy. Meanwhile, attempts to magically remove the whetstone from Thor's head ultimately failed (Sturluson, *Edda*, p. 89).

The Exploit with Geirrod

Hrungnir did seem not particularly bright, but other giants were more cunning. Geirrod was among their rank.

Loki borrowed Freyja's falcon cloak to amuse himself. He thought he might play the spy, and entered Geirrod's court in falcon shape. He was ultimately noticed and captured, and the falcon shape did not fool Geirrod. The giant starved Loki for three months, and finally extracted an oath from him in exchange for release. Loki was to bring Thor to Geirrod's court without Thor's trademark hammer and belt of strength (Sturluson, *Edda*, p. 90). There, presumably, in an indefensible position, Thor would be captured and assassinated. (Was this payback for Hrungnir?)

A friendly giantess named Grid tipped off Thor to the plot. Grid lent Thor a belt of strength, a pair of iron gloves and her staff. On his way to Geirrod's court, Thor crossed a river. The waters inexplicably rose to dangerous levels, and he was in danger of drowning! Geirrod's daughter, Gjalp, was straddling the river and causing it to rise with either her urine or menstrual fluids. Thor picked up a stone and threw it at the giantess, driving her away and ending this rather disgusting episode (Sturluson, *Edda*, pp. 90-91).

Arriving at Geirrod's court, Thor was given the indignity of lodging in goat quarters with only one chair to service him. As he sat on the chair he noticed it was rising rapidly, trying to crush him against the roof. He used Grid's staff as leverage and pushed down hard on the chair. After a severe cracking sound, he discovered Gjalp had returned, along with her sister, Greip. It was they who had taken form as the chair, but Thor had broken their backs (Sturluson, *Edda*, p. 91).

After some time, Geirrod called Thor into his hall to participate in contests. Geirrod, of course, presumed Thor was unarmed, having no idea Grid had lent him some iron gloves. The giant took some tongs from a nearby fire and threw a piece of glowing iron at Thor. Thor caught it in the iron gloves and, unscathed, returned fire at Geirrod. The giant stood behind an iron pillar in defense, but the might of Thor caused the missile to be thrown with such force that it penetrated the pillar. The pillar came crashing down, and Geirrod fell to his death (Sturluson, *Edda*, pp. 91-92).

The Dwarves' Gifts

One day Loki decided to cut off the long, flowing golden mane of Sif, Thor's wife. Thor naturally took umbrage. Loki's life would surely have ended had he not promised to arrange to get the dwarves, the renowned smiths of the Nine Worlds, to forge him a replacement gift.

13

Loki went to the sons of Ivaldi, Brokk and Eitri. Brokk, who seemed to be the leader, fashioned Sif's hair. He also threw in a spear for Odin that never missed its target (Gungnir) and a magical ship that could be folded into a pocket (Skidbladnir) (Sturluson, *Edda*, p. 92).

It could have ended there, but Loki never knew when to quit. He engineered a contest of pride between the dwarves, using his own head as collateral. He said Eitri could never fashion three items so amazing as what Brokk had just wrought. As the dwarves worked the bellows, Loki tried to interfere in the form of a biting fly. The dwarves created Draupnir, the golden ring that spawned other gold rings every nine nights; a golden boar that provided light no matter how dark it was outside; and a hammer that always hit its mark and returned to its user (Sturluson, *Edda*, p. 92-93).

The Æsir were to judge which of the various gifts was best. Odin, Thor and Freyr acted as judges. To Odin was given Draupnir, and Gungnir. Freyr received the ship and the boar. Thor was given Sif's replacement hair (the item that had started this whole enterprise) as well as the hammer, called Mjolnir. The gods judged that the hammer was the best gift of all, for Thor could use it to defend Asgard from the giants (Sturluson, *Edda*, p. 92-93).

As for Loki, with the gods declaring the hammer the best gift, he lost the wager with the dwarf. He attempted to flee but Thor caught him. Brokk demanded his head. Loki replied with a lawyer's trick, saying the dwarf could have his head but not his neck. This bit of legal wrangling did save Loki's life. However, the dwarf had a final laugh because he sewed shut Loki's lips (Sturluson, *Edda*, pp. 93-94).

Viking Age bellows-stone from Snaptun, Denmark,
showing Loki with his lips sewn shut.
National Museum of Denmark. CC BY-SA 2.0

Brokk and Eitri taking Mjolnir out of the forge, as envisioned by
artist E. Boyd Smith. Brown, *In the Days of Giants* (1902).

Poetic Kennings

We learn that poetic synonyms for Thor are:

> The son of Odin and the earth
> The father of Magni, Modi and Thrud
> The husband of Sif
> The stepfather of Ull
> The wielder or possessor of Mjolnir
> Of the mighty girdle
> Of the hall Bilskirnir
> The defender of Asgard and Midgard
> The foe and killer of giants and troll women
> The adversary of Hrungnir, Geirrod and Thrivaldi
> The lord of Thjalfi and Roskva
> The enemy of the Midgard Serpent
> The foster son of Vingnir and Hlora
>
> (Sturluson, *Edda*, pp. 109)

Silver Thor's Hammer amulet from the Viking Age.
Rømersdal, Denmark. National Museum of Denmark, CC BY-SA 2.0.

Chapter Two: The Poetic Edda

The Poetic Edda

The Poetic Edda is the single best source of North mythology at our disposal, though as a source of information it is not without its own problems.

Around 1643 Bishop Brynjólfur Sveinsson discovered a forgotten manuscript, now called the *Codex Regius* (Hollander, pp. xiii-xiv). The manuscript has been dated to 1270 CE (Larrington, p. xi), though it seems whoever was writing it down was compiling material (scribal errors included) from at least two different manuscripts (Hollander, p. xiv). Linguistic analysis has revealed the poems contain the West Norse speech of the Viking Age, and that the subject matter must have originated there (Hollander, pp. xvii-xviii).

The poems are thus "authentic" insofar as they seem to derive from the time and place of Vikings. There is however an ongoing argument as to how much outside influence they have. The *Völuspá*, for instance, a tale of the Norse cosmos from creation to destruction, may have some Christian eschatological overtones (Hollander, pp. 1-2; Tolley, p. 20; Ferguson, p. 56).

The origins of the word "Edda" is itself disputed, but one possible meaning is "poetics" (Hollander, p. xiii). Eddic poetry was simple in style, anonymous in origin, and dealt with gods and heroes (Hollander, p. xv). Skaldic poetry, by contrast, was far more complicated in style and usually composed by a named court-poet (Sturluson, *Edda*, p. x).

Thematically, the Eddic poems deal with two different subjects. The mythological poems, as one might expect, concern deities. The heroic poems speak of human beings, albeit ones from legend (Larrington, p. xi).

Below are the mythological poems in which Thor is mentioned. If I have previously described the tales in detail in the *Prose Edda* section, then I only allude to them here.

Seeress's Prophecy

In *Völuspá* (Seeress's Prophecy), Odin acts as necromancer and bids a seeress (a giantess?) rise from the grave to extoll her knowledge (Larrington, p. 3). She spins a narrative of the cosmos from primordial creation to destruction at Ragnarok. Thor is mentioned briefly in the episode of the Master Builder (Larrington, p. 7), and then his fight with the Midgard Serpent at Ragnarok (Larrington, p. 11). Both these stories are given more treatment in the *Prose Edda*.

Harbard's Song

In *Hárbarðsljóð* (Harbard's Song), Odin disguises himself as a ferryman named Harbard. He taunts his son, Thor, as to who had the greater exploits. This seems to be indicative of the tension between the aristocrats, whom Odin represented, and the commoners whom Thor championed (Larrington, p. 69).

In the boasting between these two alpha-males, many of their respective adventures are recalled, some of which are not known outside this poem. Among the exploits of Thor which are known elsewhere in Lore is his fighting of the giant Hrungnir (Larrington, p. 71), the slaying of the giant Thjazi (Larrington, p. 72), and being stuffed into a glove by the giant Utgarda-Loki (Larrington, p. 73). All these accounts are explained in detail in the *Prose Edda*. Thor is also confirmed as the son of Odin (Larrington, p. 70).

Some accounts are not otherwise known. Thor claims to have fought giant women who lived in the mountains of the east; had he not defeated them, they would have overrun mankind (Larrington, p. 73). While in the east yet again, the sons of Svárang pelted him with stones, but he managed to turn the tables on them (Larrington, p. 73). Elsewhere, Thor wrecked his ship and fought a cabal of berserker-witches who could turn themselves into she-wolves (Larrington, p. 74).

In this work, Thor takes credit for slaying Thjazi and placing the giant's eyes into the heavens as stars. However, in the *Prose Edda*, it merely says "the Æsir present" kill Thjazi, without referencing a specific individual responsible. Further, the task of placing Thjazi's eyes into the heavens is given to Odin, not Thor (Sturluson, p. 82-83).

Hymir's Poem

Hymiskviða (Hymir's Poem) recounts a famous adventure between Thor and Tyr. (Tyr may not have been the original companion to Thor in this story; there is some speculation he replaced Loki.) To facilitate a feast for the

Thor arguing with Odin in *Hárbarðsljóð*,
as envisioned by artist W. G. Collingwood.
Bray, *The Elder or Poetic Edda* (1908).

gods, Thor and Tyr must procure a cauldron from the giant Hymir, who in this version is Tyr's father (Larrington, p. 78).

Thor eats Hymir out of house and home, so they must go fishing. In the course of it, he raises the Midgard Serpent. Thor hits the creature on its head, and it falls back to the sea. Back home, an unhappy Hymir suggests Thor is not strong unless he can break his magic crystal goblet. Hymir's wife, a monstrous creature who apparently had an unhappy marriage with the giant, advises Thor to smash the goblet against Hymir's head. This he gladly does. Finally, Thor and Tyr remove the cauldron which was the cause of the adventure. On their way back, Thor spots a mob of angry giants following them, led by Hymir. Thor single-handedly dispatches them all with his hammer (Larrington, pp. 80-83).

Thor's goat collapses, half dead and lame, a gift of Loki (Larrington, p. 83). This stanza is inserted seemingly out of nowhere and doesn't seem to fit with the rest of the story. It would make more sense if Thor's original companion in this adventure was in fact Loki rather than Tyr.

Thor's encounter with Hymir is repeated in the *Prose Edda*, though with significant differences. In the *Poetic Edda*, Thor is accompanied by Tyr (possibly originally by Loki), and the fishing expedition occurs within the larger context of having to procure a cauldron for brewing. He seemingly reels in the Midgard Serpent by accident, for they were fishing simply to restock Hymir's pantry supplies which Thor had eaten. In the *Prose Edda,* by contrast, Thor

Carved stone preserved in the church at Hørdum, Denmark, showing Thor fishing for the Midgard Serpent; note that his foot has gone through the bottom of the boat. National Museum of Denmark, CC BY-SA 2.0.

makes a point to go alone, and there is no mention of the cauldron. Instead he is specifically there to find the Midgard Serpent and test his strength (Larrington, p. 63-65).

Loki's Quarrel

Lokasenna (Loki's Quarrel) is an infamous outing where Loki crashes a dinner party of the gods. Following a poetic convention, all deities present chide Loki after Loki unleashes malicious accusations maligning their characters. Loki's accusations against the gods all seem to have a measure of validity (Larrington, p. 84).

Thor is initially absent, but arrives after Loki has unleashed his share of volleys. Loki references Thor's inability to prevent his father Odin's death at Ragnarok, as well as Thor's exploits with the giant Utgarda-Loki, both of which are described in detail in the *Prose Edda*. Thor, meanwhile, promises to bash in Loki's head with the same hammer that killed the giant Hrungnir, and Loki eventually absconds (Larrington, pp. 94-95).

Thrym's Poem

Þrymskviða (Thrym's Poem) would have seemed a hilarious outing to its original audience. Our conceptions of gender in the modern West are fairly fluid, but would have been more fixed back in the day. The hilarity ensues from the ultra-masculine Thor having to crossdress as the ever-feminine Freyja.

The giant Thrym has stolen Thor's Hammer and hidden it away. Loki learns Thrym will not return it until the beautiful Freyja is given to him as a bride (Larrington, pp. 97-98). With Freyja's power and fertility in their hands, the giants would eventually predominate in their struggle against the gods (Larrington, p. 99).

Thor being dressed as a bride, as envisioned by artist E. Boyd Smith. Brown, *In the Days of Giants* (1902).

It is suggested at a council of the gods that Thor dress up as Freyja and infiltrate the giant's base. This he does (reluctantly), and the giants are amazed at the appetite displayed by "Freyja" as well as the angry fire emanating from "her" eyes (Larrington, pp. 99-100). When the hammer Mjolnir is brought in as a wedding present, Thor seizes it and unceremoniously kills Thrym and his sister (Larrington, p. 100).

All-Wise's Sayings

Alvíssmál (All-Wise's Sayings) demonstrates Thor's practical intelligence. The dwarf Alvis intends to marry Thor's daughter without the latter's knowledge or consent. Dwarves, it seem, have the unfortunate habit of turning into stone in direct sunlight. Thor continually begs Alvis to expound upon poetic synonyms of various things, which the sophomoric dwarf eagerly does, oblivious to the rising threat in the sky. After some time, in which a treasure trove of poetry is uttered, Alvis finally falls prey to Thor's stratagem (Larrington, p. 109).

The story seems to have been composed as an excuse to list poetic synonyms. Within the story, however, it is not clear why Thor resorts to this charade, rather than simply bashing the dwarf with his hammer (Hollander, p. 110). Such subterfuge is much more in line with the character of his father, Odin.

We will see in a following section, in *The Saga of Egil and Asmund,* there is at least one more occasion where Thor uses trickery rather than force to solve a problem.

Thor rescuing his daughter Thrud as the dwarf Alvis is turned to stone, as envisioned by artist W. G. Collingwood. Bray, *The Elder or Poetic Edda* (1908).

Chapter Three: Other Literature

Family Sagas

The *Íslendinga sögur*, often known in English as the "family sagas," are prose accounts of families and characters of Iceland. *Saga* comes from a Germanic word meaning "to say" (Modern High German: *sagen*). They were written down in the 13ᵗʰ and 14ᵗʰ centuries CE but concern events some three centuries or so earlier, during the age when Iceland was settled (Kellog, pp. xviii-xx). Many of the settlers are Norwegians who are fleeing the increasing centralization of King Harold Finehair's monarchy, and his usurpation of ancestral lands.

The sagas purportedly concern real places and historic personage—in this case, the wealthy farming families of Iceland. The concern with non-royal elements as well as the fact they are written in prose rather than verse distinguishes them from the formal "epics" of world literature (Kellog, p. xviii). The plot usually concerns the various feuds and legal battles between rival families and characters. Occasionally elements of what might be called "the supernatural" intrude and offer intriguing glimpses of Icelandic magic and ghost lore (Kellog, p. xxi). The gods themselves do not factor in these tales, but their presence is felt indirectly as they inspire their devotees. Many of the characters in these sagas have a theophoric ("god-bearing") "Thor" name; reading the sagas can become very confusing because of it.

There is some question as to the veracity of the sagas. They were written down three centuries after the fact. Further, the Christian audience that wrote them may not have entirely understood or appreciated Iceland's Heathen past. But the sagas at least tell us what 13ᵗʰ and 14ᵗʰ century Icelanders *told themselves* about their Heathen past. And where it concerns the supernatural, the sagas at least tell us what thirteenth century Icelanders *thought* happened in Iceland three centuries earlier (Tolley, p. 149).

Our principal interest in these Icelandic family sagas is *Eyrbyggja Saga* and *Eirik the Red's Saga*, discussed below.

Eyrbyggja Saga

In chapter three, a Norwegian character called Hrolf is described as a "close friend of Thor" and administered a temple to the god. For his services to his god, people called him Thorolf (Palsson, p. 27). A "close friend" of a deity is usually interpreted that said devotee offered the deity many sacrifices.

In chapter four, Thorolf consults his god whether he should stay and make peace with the King of Norway, or leave for Iceland. We are not told the means by which Thorolf consulted Thor, but the god advised him to seek his fortunes in Iceland. Thorolf dismantled the temple. He took onto his ship most of the temple's timber frame and some soil from under the pedestal where the cultic image stood (Palsson, p. 28).

As Thorolf entered Iceland, he cast into the waters the high seat pillars that had stood in Thor's temple. An image of the god was carved on one of these. Thorolf declared he would settle wherever the pillars landed. Immediately and quickly the pillars floated to a particular spot. Thorolf settled there, calling it Thor's Ness, and the river near it he called Thor's river. Thorolf conducted a land-taking ritual, whereby he circumambulated the land he claimed while carrying fire. On that land Thorolf established a farm and a large temple to Thor (Palsson, p. 28-29).

Chapter Four offers a very famous passage of Thor's temple in Iceland, though its veracity is suspect. Its door was in a sidewall near the gable. A structure like a church quire was within, and on it a raised altar. On the altar was a large oath ring which the priest wore at all functions, and on which people swore their oaths. The altar also contained a bowl for sacrificial blood, and a twig used to asperge the sacrificial blood. The saga says the priest's duty was to maintain the temple and hold sacrificial feasts there. The temple was supported both from the priest's private funds as well as taxes paid by farmers in the district (Palsson, p. 29).

The mountain on Thor's Ness was considered sacred. It was called Helgafell (Holy Mountain), and Thorolf believed it would house the spirits of his kinsmen when they died. Neither man nor beast was to be killed on it. Everyone had to wash themselves before treading upon it. No one could urinate or defecate on the soil—they had to use a rock which was located in the nearby sea (Palsson, p. 29-30).

The plot of the saga starts moving when an arrogant family, the Kjalleklings, no longer pays heed to the sacredness of the mountain and relieve themselves on it. Thorolf by this point is deceased, but his son, Thorstein Cod-Biter, prosecutes a feud against them (Palsson, p. 34-35).

24

Thorstein had a son, Thorgrim, dedicating him to Thor and hoping he would become a temple priest. In time, Thorstein died. It was said that Thorstein and Thorolf, as well as Thorolf's original crew from the voyage from Norway, had their souls interned in the sacred mountain of Thor where they feasted and drank together (Palsson, p. 38).

Eirik the Red's Saga

This is an amazing piece of literature, for it purportedly describes Viking Age Scandinavians discovering Vinland (America) several centuries before Columbus (Kunz, pp. 640-641). It also contains a famous passage of *oracular seidhr*, the poorly understood esoteric art by which a seeress foretold the future (Kunz, pp. 658-666). Our purpose, however, is to discuss Thor.

A party of Scandinavians set anchor on an island somewhere between Iceland and Vinland. They wintered there but did not have the foresight to bring many supplies. They attempted to hunt and fish, but this did not yield enough sustenance. Most of the crew were Christians and implored their god for help, but none seemed to be forthcoming (Kunz, pp. 667).

At this point a man named Thorhall extricated himself from the party. He went missing for three days until he was found at the edge of cliff. This strange curmudgeonly man was staring skyward, mumbling to himself and pinching himself at times. We learn later that he was composing a poem to Thor (a poem, or perhaps a spell. . . ?). In response to the poem a type of whale never before seen by the Scandinavians became beached, and the starving expedition eagerly carved it up (Kunz, pp. 667-668).

They *were* eager, that is, until they discovered Thorhall was a Heathen and that Thor had provided the whale. Thorhall claimed Thor as his guardian, calling him by his by-name, Redbeard, and declared that the god had seldom disappointed him. Thorhall taunted his Christian companions that Thor had provided whereas their savior had not. We are told the scandalized Christians threw away the whale meat and threw themselves on Christ's mercy, at which point they developed better luck finding provisions (Kunz, pp. 668).

Thorhall claimed he had given a gift to his god, Thor, and in return Thor had furnished the gift of the whale. The Christians, meanwhile, had no luck until they completely subjugated themselves to their god's mercy. In this story we can see no clearer dichotomy between Heathen theology and Christian theology: the former is based on a gift for a gift, and the latter is based on submission and blind faith.

Kristni Saga

This "Story of Conversion" shares some similarities with the family sagas, but more properly is a work of hagiography, or Christian writings concerning their saints (Grønle, pp. xxx-xxxi).

Thangbrand was a missionary to Iceland. His ship was badly thrashed at sea. A woman poet named Steinunn wrote a verse attributing the storm to Thor's displeasure.

> *Thor drew Thvinnell's animal,*
> *Thangbrand's long ship, from land,*
> *Shook the prow's horse and hit it,*
> *And hurled it against the sand.* (Grønle, p. 43)

This charming little ditty speaks to a broader picture about the religious landscape in Iceland at the beginning of the Medieval era. Thor was increasingly seen by the native Heathen population as the champion of the faith against the incursion of Christianity. More of this will be said later in the history section.

The Legendary Sagas

The *fornaldarsögur* are often known as "legendary sagas" and concern themselves with pre-Icelandic Germanic heroes (Kellog, p. xx). Elements of the supernatural are far more prevalent in these legends than in the family sagas (Kellog, p. xxi). Most of these sagas date from the 14th and 15th centuries, but at least a few are based squarely on older material. To what extent these sagas exist as a true literary genre is debated by academics (Driscoll, pp. 71-72), but that doesn't concern us here.

We will look at three of these: *Gautrek's Saga, The Saga of Egil and Asmund,* and *Thorstein-Mansion Might's Story.*

Gautrek's Saga

One day, in an episode that seems somewhat similar to Agamemnon and Iphigenia of Greek myth, King Vikar finds he has lost divine favor. There is no wind to power the sails of his naval fleet, and his army is stranded. Divination reveals that Odin, chieftain of the gods, wants a human sacrifice. Lots are drawn, and Vikar himself is chosen (Odin, god of kings, had a habit of sacrificing his own).

Starkad is a great warrior and counselor to King Vikar. In response to this dire demand to sacrifice the king, his foster-father, Grani Horse-hair, leads him away to a meeting of men. It is soon revealed that Grani is a guise for Odin himself.

Starkad finds that those assembled are discussing not the king's fate, but his own. A verbal sparring match occurs between Odin and his son Thor concerning Starkad. The rivalry seemingly started with the fact that Starkad's mother chose to procreate with Odin rather than Thor himself. Thor and Odin dole out curses and blessings that seem to counter each other. This goes on for some time until finally the men assembled agreed that Starkad shall bear the brunt of every blessing and curse that had been uttered by the dueling gods.

Odin demands that Starkad repay him for the help he received in dealing with Thor, and Starkad agrees. Starkad then returns to the messy situation with King Vikar and his impending sacrifice. Starkad tries to arrange a mock sacrifice where Vikar is not actually killed, but through Odin's subterfuge and magic Vikar ultimately does die. One cannot cheat Odin of his due (Waggoner, pp. 19-24).

The sparring match between Odin and Thor is reminiscent of the rivalry between them in *Harbard's Song* from the *Poetic Edda*, and speaks to the same tensions between their respective cults. Starkad is a heroic warrior, a king's counselor and a member of the nobility. As such, he is Odin's. One of Thor's curses is that Starkad would be hated by the common people; after King Vikar dies in the supposed mock sacrifice, this curse comes true (Waggoner, p. 21).

The Saga of Egil and Asmund

Two young, legendary warriors named and Egil and Asmund encounter each other. After testing each other in combat and athleticism, and declaring their mutual admiration for each other, they decide to become sworn brothers (Palsson and Edwards, p. 95).

The two meet a giantess and her daughter named, respectively, Eagle-Beak and Skin-Beak. The two warriors accept an offer of hospitality from the giantess. They decide to trade life stories while dinner is cooking (Palsson and Edwards, p. 97). The adventures of Egil and Asmund make for interesting reading, but we will concentrate only on Eagle-Beak's story as it concerns Thor.

Eagle-Beak (*Arinnefja*) was one of eighteen daughters of the giant Oskrud, and she was widely considered the prettiest among them. Oskrud and his wife died; Oskrud's brothers stole most of the inheritance. All that was left to the daughters was a gold ring. Meanwhile, Eagle-Beak claims she became the abused servant of her other sisters. After a period of being bullied by her sisters, she made a pact with Thor. She would give him any goat he wanted if he were to handle the matter (Palsson and Edwards, pp. 108-109).

One might imagine Thor simply using his hammer to strike down his foes, but here he chose to employ a bit of mischief. Thor's stratagem was to sleep with every sister, starting with the eldest. This caused such jealously in the other sisters that each of the sisters he slept with was in turn killed by the others. Finally, only Eagle-Beak was left standing, and she inherited what was left of the family fortune. However, the other sisters had lain a curse that the progeny of Thor and a giantess would neither grow nor thrive; the daughter Skin-Beak was thus afflicted. Eagle-Beak also suffered the rest of her life from an insatiable sexual appetite after sleeping with Thor (Palsson and Edwards, p. 109). This amusing tale seems like it should have Odin rather than Thor as the antagonist, for trickery and seduction or more his style than Thor's. But Thor is Odin's son, and seems to have learned a thing or two from his old man.

We may care to ask why giant women in this tale find Thor a handsome stranger to bed rather than a foe to be fought. One is tempted to muse on the possible subject of "Bad Boy appeal" between gods and giants. . . .

Thorstein Mansion-Might's Story

Thorstein is the tallest and strongest man in Norway, so big he can barely fit through doors to even large houses. The latter trait gives him his sobriquet of "Mansion-Might" (Palsson and Edwards, p. 123).

Thorstein journeys to the underworld via an elf mound after putting on a pair of gloves and a magic stick. There he steals a priceless ring from an elf king and kills several of the king's retainers before escaping (Palsson and Edwards, pp. 123-125).

Thorstein encounters a dwarf whose child has been captured by a giant eagle. Thorstein kills the eagle and rescues the dwarf's child. In return the dwarf gifts Thorstein with several treasures, including a marble capable of producing both hail and fire (Palsson and Edwards, pp. 125 -126).

Thorstein treads into giant land, hiding in an oak tree while he conducts surveillance on its denizens. They are taller than he is (Palsson and Edwards, p. 127). He soon finds himself in the hall of the king, Geirrod. Thorstein engages in various brutal athletic contests, as well as drinking games (Palsson and Edwards, pp. 131-133). Eventually Thorstein kills king Geirrod by using the flames of his magic marble (Palsson and Edwards, p. 136-

137). Thorstein then becomes baptized, marries into nobility, and becomes a chieftain (Palsson and Edwards, pp. 138-140).

Toasts to Thor and Odin in this tale are mentioned (Palsson and Edwards, p. 135), but Thorstein might be himself a euhemerized version of Thor.

Heimskringla

Snorri Sturluson, the presumed author of the *Prose Edda,* also wrote a history of the Norse kings, *Heimskringla* ("circle of the world"). This "historical saga" is a collection of biographies in which the author tries to relate all details to the overall story (Sturluson, *Heimskringla,* pp. xv-xvi). This purported history begins with the mythological figures of the gods that we find in the *Eddas;* here they are euhemerized into priest-kings and priestess-queens who are considered nearly divine because of their magic. The early chapters necessarily involve supernatural elements around these figures.

As the biographies progress and approach closer to Snorri's own time they become less supernatural and more historical. The supernatural, however, still intrudes at times. For example, Odin makes an appearance in the story of King Olav Tryggvason, where the All-Father tries (unsuccessfully) to feed the Christian king some enchanted (poisoned?) sacrificial meat (Sturluson, *Heimskringla,* pp. 167-168).

As far as Thor, the two main sections of *Heimskringla* under concern are *Ynglinga Saga* and *Hakon the Good.*

Ynglinga Saga

As mentioned, the gods are reduced to human magicians who are worshipped as divine because of their incredible magical abilities. Odin's tribe is originally from west Asia. Much of the saga concerns Odin's abilities, personality and exploits (Sturluson, *Heimskringla,* pp. 1-4). Thor is mentioned merely as one of Odin's kin and fellow magician-priests (*díar*); he held his estate in the land of Thrudvang (Sturluson, *Heimskringla,* p. 4). Odin's and Thor's names inspired several personal names in their lands (Sturluson, *Heimskringla,* p. 7).

History of Hakon the Good

We are treated to a purported tale of Heathen blood sacrifice, or *blót,* in Norway. The client farmers of the district would bring all their eatables to the temple and were provided with ale. Cattle and horses were slaughtered, and their flesh was cooked to be eaten on kettles that hung over fires. The blood of the sacrificial animals (*hlaut*) was collected in *hlaut*-bowls, and the temple walls inside and out were sprinkled with said blood, as were the participants. The presiding officiant of the sacrifice blessed the blood and the flesh. Three bowls were set out for the gods—one to Odin for victory in war, and one each to Freyr and Nord for prosperity and peace. There was also a bowl for Bragi, the poet, and one for the honored dead (Sturluson, *Heimskringla*, p. 87).

Needless to say, all of the above would have been considered scandalous by Medieval Christians. King Hakon had accepted Christianity and was advised by English clergy (Sturluson, *Heimskringla*, p. 86). Hakon tried to establish Christianity as the law of the land. But the citizens of Trondheim, Norway's seat of power, were inherently "conservative" in the true sense of the word—resistant to change. Behind this conservatism lay a theological presumption that the bounty of the land and fecundity of the seasons depended on the king performing sacrifices on behalf of the community. If kings no longer acted in their sacral capacity of offering blood sacrifice to the gods, then the gods would withhold their favor. Everything from bad luck to starvation would ensue (Sturluson, *Heimskringla*, pp. 87-89).

At a Winter's Day feast, Hakon was to perform a sacrifice. He was counseled by his advisor, a jarl (earl) named Sigurd, that despite his Christian reservations, Hakon should go through the motions of a Heathen sacrifice lest there be an uproar among the people. This leads to a somewhat comical episode. Sigurd blesses the offering bowl to Odin and then toasts the king over a ritual horn. When the horn is in turn handed to Hakon, the Christian king makes the sign of the Cross over it. When one of the farmer citizens present questions what the king is doing, Sigurd the Jarl does damage control and claims the king was signing himself with Thor's Hammer (Sturluson, *Heimskringla*, p. 88).

This passage has been debated by modern Heathens. Making the sign of the hammer as a hallowing gesture is popular in modern Heathenry. Is the passage above proof there was a Hammer ritual, or was Sigurd just being a glib politician and wholesale inventing a tradition to cover up his boss's social *faux paus*?

Skaldic Poetry

Skaldic poetry has been mentioned in passing as a contrast to Eddic poetry. Whereas Eddic poetry is relatively simple and anonymous, Skaldic poetry is composed by a known court poet (*skald*), and is far more complicated in style. One of the defining features of skaldic poetry is its unlimited use of *kennings* (Hollander, p. xxii). A kenning is a "condensed metaphorical expression" with a "real, or implied, comparison" (Hollander, p. xxi). Because of its liberal use of kennings, skaldic poetry can be incomprehensible to anyone not versed in the art.

Thor is mentioned at times by several skalds; his exploits with the giants were suitable fodder for poetic expression (Turville-Petre, p. 84-85). We will look to *Thorsdrapa* below as the principal example.

Þórsdrápa

Around 985 CE, the skald Eilifr Godrunarson composed a poem, *Thorsdrapa* (*Þórsdrápa*, Thor's Praise-Poem) on behalf of his patron, Earl Hakon of Hladir. The poet takes elaborative use of kennings to new and dizzying heights.

Godrunarson retells the story of Thor and the giant Geirrod, but makes some notable changes from Snorri's version, including adding the figure of Thjalfi at Thor's side. Thor's martial exploits are heavily praised. In writing this work, it seems Thor has become a poetic cipher for Earl Hakon, while the figure of Thjalfi is stand-in for the poet himself ("Eulogy on Thor").

This indirect praise poem can tell us something about how court poets operated in 10th century Norway. For our purposes, however, what matters is that when a court poet needed a mythological cipher for martial valor, he turned to Thor.

Summary of Lore

Our literary sources on this Heathen god have the misfortune of being written down by Christians sometime after conversion. In certain instances we are left wondering if what is said is reflective of reality, or a distortion caused by time and differing worldviews. On the whole, however, the literary sources reveal a consistent picture of Thor.

Thor is the strongest of the gods. He never backs down from a fight or a challenge and is ever willing to test his might and main. Odin's stratagems and Loki's duplicities often cause headaches for the gods, and usually Thor must threaten Loki before Loki rectifies the matter. Thor's usual methods for dealing with problems are courage and strength, but in at least two encounters Thor resorts to cunning.

Thor is Odin's eldest son and (with the possible exception of Balder) his most prized offspring. Father and son fight and die together at Ragnarok.

And yet there is a certain tension between the two resulting in their differing personalities and proclivities. The tensions presumably spill over into their respective cults, the aristocrats versus the peasants.

Thor is implacable in battle but not cruel. Aside from some occasional spats with his father and occasional annoyances at Loki, he seems to get along well with the other beings of Asgard. He is, in the most part, fair to human beings, and the lore speaks of devoted followers. The tales of Thorhall and Thorolf nicely summarize Heathen theology: those who are friends of Thor and give him gifts or sacrifices can expect his favor in return.

Thor is a mighty defender, but also a hallowing force. The two are inseparable. The hammer Mjolnir, covered as it sometimes is in the blood and brains of foes, also consecrates and hallows in matters of life and death.

Amber carving of a male figure gripping his long plaited or twisted beard, thought to represent Thor. Fedet, Roholte, Denmark.
National Museum of Denmark, CC BY-SA 2.0.

PART II: HISTORY

Part Two offers a general history lesson that serves as a background to Heathenry for those who may lack it. These historical sections are necessarily abbreviated—I am writing a devotional work, not a dissertation. I have tried to highlight what I feel best serves an historical understanding of Thor's cults.

We begin with the proto-Indo-European antecedents of Heathenry. We then survey in turn the principle topographical and chronological areas of Heathenry where Thor was honored—the Continent, Anglo-Saxon England, and Viking Age Scandinavia. The historical era will end with a quick glance at Thor's connection with runes and the symbol of the *swastika*, and a look at his role in the Pennsylvania German tradition of Urglaawe.

Some of the problems in the academic study of Heathenry will soon become apparent. The continental section betrays the fact most of the commentators were outsiders—Romans or Christians. The paucity of the Anglo-Saxon section betrays the dearth of sources on that era. Most of our knowledge on Thor does come from the Scandinavian sources, though these sources are often filtered through hostile Christian lenses.

Nonetheless, taken as a whole, it is evident that Thor (or by whatever name he was locally known) was a major deity in all eras of Heathenry. He was popular with warriors, farmers and even runic magicians. His main function is his defensive strength for which he can be called upon in many instances to protect and to hallow.

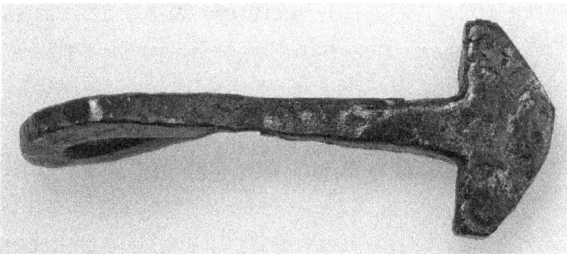

Simple Thor's Hammer amulet forged from iron. Birka, Uppland, Sweden. Swedish Historical Museum 914272. CC BY 2.5 SE.

Chapter Four: The Proto-Indo-Europeans

A Slice of the PIE

Many languages, from the tip of the Iberian peninsula to the Indian subcontinent, are related through a common root language called proto-Indo-European (PIE) (Mallory, p. 22). The original proto-Indo-Europeans had a home somewhere in Eurasia; its exact location is disputed (Mallory, p. 144-145), but a likely hypothesis places it somewhere in the Pontic-Caspian Sea region (Mallory, p. 122). PIE society was patrilineal and patriarchal (Mallory, p. 123), centered around home and clan (Mallory, p. 124), and its economy centered on livestock, particularly cattle (Mallory, p. 117). It was operative from around 4000-2500 BCE (Mallory, p. 145).

Throughout the various descendant Indo-European cultures, there are a few reoccurring mythological motifs which are presumed to originate from the original PIE religion. Among these motifs are creation of the world through sacrifice (Mallory, p. 140), and a war between differing tribes of deities or different functions of society (Mallory, p. 139). We can see this PIE influence in Norse polytheism: Odin and his brothers sacrificed Ymir to create the world (Sturluson, *Edda*, p. 16), while the Æsir and Vanir fought each other before they were reconciled (Sturluson, *Edda*, pp. 33-34). We also see the PIE influence in Heathenry as the god known as Tyr/Tiw/Tiwaz bears a linguistic resemblance to Zeus and Jupiter (Turville-Petre, p. 182), all these deities presumably the cultural descendants of the Indo-European Shining Sky Father (Mallory, p. 129).

As for Thor, some PIE scholars see him as akin to the Indo-European "striker" god, *Perkuno* (Mallory, pp. 129, 141). *Perkuno was a hero god, a champion. As god of thunder, he gave life-giving rains and was a friend to the farmers. But as god of lightning, he also fought with demons who embodied chaos, often depicted as a serpent or dragon. He was associated with mountains and oaks, carried a special weapon, and was noted for gluttony (Serith, "Proto-Indo-European Deities"). While Thor certainly fits this role in a mythological sense, his name is not linguistically cognate to other deities thought to play this role in other cultures. However, *Fjörgyn*, one of the names of the mother of Thor, may (Mallory, p. 129).

Perhaps on the broadest level, the greatest legacy of PIE religion to its descendant cultures was its theology.

Giving and Getting a Slice of the PIE

The theological presumption of PIE religion, which was inherited by the various descendant religions, can be summed up in the word *ghostis*. *Ghostis* embodies within it a sense of host-guest relations. The exchange of gifts is seen as the mechanism by which human beings and their supernatural benefactors interact with each other (Serith, "What Was Proto-Indo-European Religion Like?").

Recent converts to paganism from other religions are sometimes mystified by this simple theology. The three Abrahamic faiths view religion as a complete submission to an omnipotent, omniscient supreme being. He enforces a stern and detailed code of morality. Straying from this ethical path makes one impure, and—in Islam and Christianity, at least—conveys the risk of eternal damnation of one's soul. Followers of eastern religions, meanwhile, often see the point of their religions as following an ethical guide to attain a supreme enlightenment and/or break an eternal cycle of rebirth and suffering in the material world.

PIE religion shared neither of these premises with the Abrahamic or Eastern faiths. Instead the spiritual interactions between human beings and the unseen forces was not unlike the human social interactions of early PIE society itself. Individuals and groups were united by a system of exchange. To entreat a group or individual, another group or individual gave them something of value. This gift obligated the other party to give something back (Serith, "What Was Proto-Indo-European Religion Like?"). And so was born the idea of *a gift for a gift*.

But the nature of the gift was determined by the status of the one giving it. The poor and powerless did not have much means to give, but those with the means to give more were expected to do so. Thus, a clan leader would have been expected to render a more valuable gift than a serf. And how much more so were the expectations of a god's gift compared to that of a clan leader? (Thomas, "The Nature of Sacrifice")

In practice this meant religion was a matter of *sacrifice*. Sacrifice, in the original sense of the word, meant to *make sacred*. Material objects were set aside from the world of daily affairs and ritualistically given to the gods and spirits, as gifts. In return, the gods and spirits were expected to convey boons that were in their power to give (Thomas, "The Nature of Sacrifice"). In those days, the most sought-after boons would have been very practical affairs for the survival and maintenance of the clan—*e.g.*, wealth, prosperity, a good harvest, health, a successful childbirth, and military victory.

Many generations later, these concerns were still largely what the average person in society needed to survive. And the descendant cultures of the Proto-Indo-Europeans still largely understood religion as means by which the individual or community entreated their supernatural benefactors through ritual sacrifice, the act of reciprocity.

The Romans, for instance, refined their religion into a very legalistic mindset. The rituals were to be done in a precise, almost pedantic manner, ensuring the correct deities received the correct offerings at the correct time of year and in the correct places. The heart of Roman theology was expressed in the maxim *do ut des,* which loosely translates as "I give so that you may give" (Thomas, "The Nature of Sacrifice"). The Romans created a vast empire that spanned three continents and was the most advanced culture in the ancient West. Yet their religious presumptions, by and large, still echoed the basic formula of the primitive PIE people from the Eurasian steppes thousands of years earlier. *A gift for a gift.*

Stone head of a "boat axe" (*båtøks*), typical of the Single Grave or Battle-Axe Culture (ca. 2800 BCE), thought to have been the earliest speakers of an Indo-European language in Scandinavia. Veden, Østfold, Norway. Kulturhistorisk Museet, University of Oslo, C20376. CC BY-SA 4.0.

Chapter Five: Continental Heathenry

The Indo-Europeans spread throughout the Eurasian peninsula. As groups split off from each other, and as they encountered (or conquered) other peoples, their language and religion evolved to the languages and religions of the descendant cultures (Mallory, pp. 258-259).

The developments of the Bronze Age do not really concern us here. We will simply note that some interesting Scandinavian rock carvings have god figures carrying what seem to be axes or hammers (Davidson, pp. 80). There may be an embryo of Thor in such representations (*Our Troth*, pp. 49-50).

Rise of the Germans

At around 500 BCE a recognizably Germanic language begins to appear from the Indo-European (Mallory, p. 87). Here, then, we can begin talking of a Germanic religion—of Heathenry. And it is this criterion—language, not later and dubious European conceptions of "race"—that defines Germanic peoples. The Germanic peoples came to settle along the Rhine and intrude into Celtic territories.

Bronze Age rock art from Lövåsen, Bohuslän, Sweden: a hammer-wielding male figure, possibly an early version of Thor. Photo by Erlend Bjørtvedt, Wikimedia Commons, CC BY-SA 3.0.

A Very Brief History of Germans and Romans

The Romans eventually conquered the Celts, aside from the fringe areas such as Ireland and Scotland. But prior to that, the Germans seem to have adopted the institution of the *comitatus,* warband or armed retinue, from the Celts (Enright, pp. 200-201). The warband would have major consequences for Germanic society. As an institution, its influence would eventually eclipse older tribal assemblies (Enright, p. 195).

The Germans raided Roman and Celtic lands for some time, but were eventually subdued west of the Rhine. Roman imperial propaganda soon dreamed of an "empire without end" stretching across the world. It was not to be, however. A devastating defeat of three Roman legions at Teutoburg Forest halted the Roman advance. However, it's a fair question as to whether or not the Roman rulers, despite their official propaganda, considered the Germans and their primitive culture east of the Rhine actually worth conquering (Heather, p. 5).

Over the following generations Rome developed a complicated relationship with Germanic tribes. Trading relations were established (Heather, p. 73). Rome sent bronze drinking vessels, along with fine glassware, silverware and weapons; these prestige goods most likely were imported by German aristocrats (Todd, pp. 90-92, 95-96). German exports to Rome included amber products, agricultural products and slaves (Todd, p. 97). Rome propped up friendly tribes with diplomatic "gifts" (Heather, p. 84, Todd, p. 90). Rome benefited from the relationship by having semi-dependable allies, while the military elite in said tribes grew wealthy and influential from Roman largesse. Many Germans served in the Roman legions, either willingly or forced by treaties (Heather, pp. 74-75). Germans increasingly filled out the officer ranks of the Roman Empire, and the ones who became successfully acclimated to imperial service showed little inclination to return to their former lives as tribesmen (Todd, pp. 59-61).

Rome's political, military and economic influence over the neighboring tribes was considerable, and inspired the tribes to compete with each over to better capitalize on Roman wealth (Heather, p. 142). It also seems to have led to an increased militarization of the Germanic peoples (Heather, pp. 89-90). Old tribes disintegrated, new tribes formed, and these new tribes recruited their military manpower from a broader base of society than the old military elite of the *comitatus*. The manpower of these new tribes was better able to fend off the Roman military and plunder Roman wealth (Heather, pp. 171-172).

New tribes like the Franks and Visigoths were better able to challenge Rome on Roman territory. This time, however, the tribes had come not merely to plunder wealth and retreat, but to migrate into Roman territory (Heather, p. 205). New Germanic kingdoms emerged on the back of a dying Roman empire. In so doing, the tribes were effectively "Romanized"—taking on the forms of Roman imperial administration, vernacular forms of Latin, and Christianity.

Sources for Continental Heathenry

Unfortunately, the Heathen Germans were themselves functionally illiterate. While runes were developed sometime between 50 CE and 200 CE (Pollington, *Runes*, p. 71), these were used for laconic inscriptions on hard materials. The early Germans did not write down their history or religion for posterity.

Our knowledge of early Heathenry comes largely from the literate cultures of classical society—the Greeks and the Romans. The science of comparative anthropology was still two millennia in the future, so the classical authors had no scientific basis with which to objectively assess these alien cultures. Nor would they have been well disposed to treat them fairly, even if they had the means to do so—the Romans were often at war with the Germans. Thus, when we read the words of classical authors, we must place them into critical context.

It should be mentioned that early Germans along the Rhine were in contact with an older and somewhat more developed Celtic culture. While the Celts did not dominate the Germans, there was cultural interaction between them. The early Romans could not always distinguish between the two groups (Enright, p. 197). Thus, when the early Romans speak of the Germans, how "German" were some of these tribes, really?

The material remains of the early Germans are another source of information. Archaeology has developed as a credible science, but artefacts are still open to interpretation. However, when archeology seems to confirm the texts of classical authors, then we may presume a certain validity.

Caesar and Tacitus

Julius Caesar, writing in the middle of the first century BCE, claimed the Germans knew no divinities as such; they merely worshipped the sun, moon and fire. He also said they did not concern themselves greatly with sacrifice. From what we know of later Germanic polytheism, and from what we know of earlier PIE religion, these observations seem unlikely, at best.

Again, Caesar was an outsider and military general at war with the Germans who had no motive for objectively observing them. Caesar also claims the tribes had no priestly class, which he contrasts with the influence that the Druids held over the Celts (Caesar, pp. 344-347). Later writers do mention Germanic priests of some sort, although they probably did not understand these priests in the same terms as the Celts understood the Druids.

The Roman historian Tacitus writing about 150 years later offers a far different perspective. He says the Germans claim a Tuisto as their divine progenitor, an earth god. This god had a son called Mannus, and Mannus in turn gave birth to three eponymous gods that would lend their names to tribes: Ingaevones, Herminones, and Istaveones. Other tribes, perhaps scurrilously, also claimed different divine progenitors from Mannus. In any case, the Germans derive their name from a particularly frightening tribe which was the first to cross the Rhine and conquer Gallic territory (Tacitus, pp. 130-133).

Tacitus mentions that the Germans worshipped a set of divinities which he likens to Roman gods through the *Interpretatio Romana*, the Roman understanding of equating foreign deities to their own. These divinities are Mercury, Mars and Hercules. Some Germans knew a female divinity that Tacitus equates to Isis, and another confederation of tribes honored a deity called Nerthus, whom Tacitus likened to Terra Mater, Mother Earth (Tacitus, pp. 142-145, 196-197).

"Mercury" was their chief deity and is almost certainly the god we now know as Odin (Davidson, p. 54). Mercury was appeased through the peculiar observance of human sacrifice (at least on certain festivals). "Mars" is thought to be Tyr in an earlier, more war-like incarnation (Davidson, pp. 56-57), Hercules and his club is thought to be how Romans interpreted Thor and his hammer. His native name in this time period is "Donar"— "Donnarstag" or "Donar's Day" still being the modern German word for Thursday (Thor's Day) (Joe, "Teutonic Deities"). "Mars" and "Hercules" were honored with good old-fashioned animal sacrifice. Tacitus also claims the Germans sung of this Hercules when they were about to go into battle (Tacitus, pp. 132-133).

Tacitus says the Germans had sacred groves, and emblems and figures housed in these groves were carried into battle before the armies. He mentions the Germans had some type of officials acting as priests, who alone held the power of capital punishment. The priests conducted divinations for important affairs in peace and war by either casting lots, interpreting the flights of birds, listening to the neighing of horses kept in their sacred groves, or having captured prisoners of war fight each other. When the kings held council through tribal assemblies, it was the priests who commanded silence from the throngs (Tacitus, pp. 144-149).

Tacitus mentions that elder males acted as priests and diviners for their own household cult. Women, however, offered important support to their men in combat—imploring from the sidelines, and tending to wounds. Women in general were also thought to have special powers of insight and prophecy. Within living memory of Tacitus' own time, a female oracle by name of Veleda was treated as almost divine (Tacitus, pp. 142-143).

Tacitus might not have visited Germania and seen it with his own eyes, fashioning his narrative of Germanic tribes from second hand accounts. Further, he was a Roman politician with an agenda. Historians therefore caution us to accept Tacitus' account with a grain of salt. However, unlike Caesar's writing, Tacitus' writing on Germanic religion seems to be generally in line with what came afterward (later Heathenry). Archaeology also confirms the presence of sacrifice, even human sacrifice, to the major gods (Davidson, pp. 55-56). It is safe to say Tacitus' account is probably correct in the very broad strokes, if not always in detail.

Old Saxon Baptismal Vow

In the ninth century a baptismal vow was written in either Old Saxon or Old Dutch. The person who was about to receive baptism had to recite the vow, which stated "I renounce all the deeds and words of the devil, Thunaer, Woden and Saxnot, and all those fiends that are their companions" ("Old Saxon Baptismal Vow").

Who "Saxnot" is has frustrated scholars for some time, but that does not concern us here. Woden is Odin, and Thunaer is a Saxon version of Thor. This confirms once again that Thor was an important deity in the local Heathen religion—important enough that those seeking to be baptized to Christianity had to foreswear allegiance to him, alongside the "devil."

Jupiter Columns and Jupiter's Oak

According to the *Interpretatio Romana*, Thor could sometimes be equated to Hercules. Both were hero gods, beloved of the people, who used distinctive weapons (a hammer and a club, respectively). However, Thor could also be equated with Jupiter, for both were thundering gods of the sky.

Roman military units stationed in Britain had honored a Romano-Celtic deity called Jupiter-Taranis, a syncretic mix of the Gaulish god of thunder with Jupiter (Branston, pp. 105-106). Perhaps this expedited the identification of Thunor to Jupiter.

In Gaul, there was also the phenomenon of so-called Jupiter Columns. "Jupiter" is here depicted as an equestrian god, striking down serpentine giants with a thunderbolt. These sculptures are mounted on tall, decorative columns. Jupiter was rarely depicted by Romans on horseback. In these distinctive images there may be an echo of Thor riding his goats into battle, striking at the giants with lightning ("Iovi Optimo Maximo").

As was relayed in Tacitus, Germanic polytheists worshiped in sacred groves where they housed images and figurines of the god. One such grove seems to have survived until the eighth century, when it was destroyed by an Anglo-Saxon missionary. St. Boniface reports he destroyed a sacred tree, a *robur iovis* (Jupiter's Oak) in what is now Hesse, Germany ("Of Oaks and Axes"). Oaks, we recall, were associated with a variety of Indo-European "Striker" gods. If Jove sometimes equals Thor, then we have a lot of circumstantial evidence that this was a cultic site to a version of Thor.

Boniface chopping down "Jupiter's Oak" at Geismar in Hesse, Germany.
Shea, *Pictorial Lives of the Saints*, 1922.

Chapter Six: Anglo-Saxon England

Roman Britain

By the dawn of history, various tribes, most of which are considered Celtic, were inhabiting the island of Britain. It was invaded by Julius Caesar in the first century BCE, but was not fully conquered by the Romans until a century later, when they turned it into the province of Britannia. Even then, "conquered" might be an overstatement—the Romans eventually conceded that the northern portion of it (present day Scotland) was beyond their ability to occupy (Faulkner, "Overview"; Johnson, "Timeline").

It took four legions to pacify a relatively small piece of real estate like Britain, and three legions were retained to keep order. Boudica's rebellion in the year 60 or 61 proved that not everyone accepted the new state of affairs. When the Romans finally snuffed out the Druid order in Anglesey, imperial rule seemed to have stabilized a bit. Still, there is a question as to how much Britain was truly Romanized outside their stronghold of Londinium in the southeast (Faulkner, "Overview"; Johnson, "Timeline").

In the later empire, Britain played a role in the various political intrigues and civil wars of the western Roman Empire. It was increasingly subject to raids by Germanic peoples, whom the sources refer to as Saxons. A series of coastal defenses, called the Saxon Shore Forts, were erected to deal with the threat. Meanwhile, in the fourth century, in what is called the Barbarian Conspiracy or Great Conspiracy, rebellious Romans in Britain seemingly opened the proverbial door to a combined invasion of Saxons and Scots. The marauders swept through the land, raping and pillaging, until Roman authorities from the Continent managed to restore order (Faulkner, "Overview"; Johnson, "Timeline").

Sub-Roman Britain

In the early 400s CE, as the western Roman Empire deteriorated, what was left of the imperial administration decided the troublesome island was no longer worth retaining. Romans in Britain were told to look to their own defenses (Heather, p. 278).

In this shadowy dark age, history is sketchy and unreliable. Local warlords seemed to have replaced centralized government. According to later sources, a local king called Vortigern invited Saxons to be settled in Britain in exchange for defense against other barbarian tribes. The Saxon leader, Hengist, promptly rebelled shortly after settlement. So began a series of invasions (Mark, "Vortigern").

In the early 500s the Saxon advance seems to have temporarily halted as a result of some Romano-British victory. The legends of King Arthur arise from that era. In the end, however, the Saxon advance could not be denied. By 600 CE all of lowland Britain was conquered (Heather, pp. 279-280).

Anglo-Saxon England

The Angles, the Jutes and the Saxons most probably originated in northern Germany (Blair, p. 9). Tacitus refers to the Anglii as part of a religious confederation that honored Nerthus, the Germanic earth mother (Tacitus, pp. 196-197). Later Roman writers refer to Saxons, though it is not clear if they were a distinct people or if "Saxon" was a general termed used for differing Germanic-speaking tribesmen (Blair, p. 6; Todd, pp. 216-217). The Angles, Saxons and Jutes shared broadly in culture and language (Blair, p. 4).

There were too few Anglo-Saxons to completely wipe out the existing population (a process now referred to as "ethnic cleansing") (Heather, pp. 268-269). Instead, the invaders became the new landowning class and re-ordered the means of property wealth (Heather, pp. 293, 301). Unlike on the Continent, the invaders did not take to speaking a form of vernacular Latin: instead the native population adapted to their new overlords, and soon began speaking Anglo-Saxon (Heather, p. 302, 304).

By about 600 CE, there were at least twelve kingdoms and subkingdoms in Anglo-Saxon Britain (Blair, p. 199). These kingdoms had a complicated relationship of alliances and wars. Eventually many of these kingdoms would fall to later invasions from the Vikings.

Most of the Anglo-Saxon kingdoms were converted to Christianity by Continental missionaries by the year 700 CE. When we speak of Anglo-Saxon Heathenry, we therefore speak of a period of only three centuries—from about 400 CE at earliest to the conversion period of 700 CE. Given the divided nature of England at the time, Anglo-Saxon Heathenry seems to have been a mostly local affair. There was no central court to promote a unified paganism.

Our knowledge of Anglo-Saxon Heathenry is scant indeed. Aside from runes, the Heathens were themselves illiterate, becoming literate only with conversion to Christianity. As far as the two or three centuries from the fall of Rome to the rise of the Anglo-Saxon kingdoms, the native Britons themselves were distracted by constant warfare. One of our main sources for Anglo-Saxon religion and history, Bede, was writing in the 700s, and is somewhat removed from many of the events he describes.

In general, knowledge of Anglo-Saxon Heathenry comes from a few surviving texts and archeological remains, as well as place names.

Thunor

Thunor is the Old English word for thunder (Pollington, *The Elder Gods*, p. 199). This is very similar to the Old Saxon or Old Dutch *Thunaer*, the god who was mentioned in the Old Saxon Baptismal vow we saw earlier. As mentioned earlier, Thor and Jupiter were sometimes conflated in the *Interpretatio Romana*. In England the Roman day of the week, *dies Jovis* or Day of Jove (Jupiter), became *thunresdaeg*, or Thunor's Day (Pollington, *The Elder Gods*, p. 199).

Several place names in England contain a Thunor element (Pollington, *The Elder Gods*, p. 200). Some of these places contain the element of *–leah*, or woodland clearing, and it does bear mentioning that the continental cult of Thor was connected with sacred groves (Branston, p. 110).

The Gosforth Cross in Cumberland, England, depicts several scenes from Norse mythology, one of which is a clear reference to Thor's fishing expedition with the Midgard Serpent. The cross dates to around 900 CE and is done in the manner

Stone from Gosforth churchyard, Cumbria, England, showing Thor and Hymir fishing with an ox head. Early 10th century. Stephens, *Professor S. Bugge's Studies on Northern Mythology* (1883).

of Anglo-Saxon crosses. However, its time period places it within the era of Viking settlement of northern England. Whether it is genuinely Anglo-Saxon or Viking is hard to say (Branston, p. 116).

One interesting theory makes Thor vicariously the main protagonist of the greatest work of Old English literature. The eponymous hero of *Beowulf* is, like Thor, a champion who slays monsters with bravery and strength. That Beowulf ultimately dies from wounds in his fight with a dragon recalls Thor's death at Ragnarok from poison sprayed by the World Serpent. Is Beowulf's character an homage to Thor? Is Beowulf perhaps an euhemerized Thor, forced to take human form because Christianity could not countenance an overt reference to a Heathen deity? (Pollington, *The Elder Gods*, pp. 203-204)

As can be seen, given the paucity of evidence, there are not many striking examples of Thor/Thunor worship in the Anglo-Saxon period. To truly understand his cult, we must look at Scandinavia.

Silver penny of the Anglo-Scandinavian ruler Regnald I of York, 919-921 CE, showing Thor's Hammer with three circles (meaning unclear).
Portable Antiquities Scheme, British Museum, NLM-F304C3. CC BY-SA 4.0.

Chapter Seven: Scandinavia and the Viking Age

Ancient Scandinavia

By ancient "Scandinavia" we mean Denmark, Norway and Sweden. Iceland was colonized later.

Around 8000 BCE as the Ice Age glaciers began receding in Northern Europe, groups of hunter-gatherers moved into Scandinavia. Later waves of migration brought agriculture, bronze and then later iron tool making, and life in villages (Haywood, pp. 18-19). Denmark and southern Sweden generally had the best farmland, thus encouraging development in those areas (Haywood, p. 17).

Due to their illiteracy, the early Scandinavia peoples left no indigenous historical accounts. Archaeology and Roman sources, however, provide a clear picture of influence from Rome as it expanded. The Romans traded with these peoples, and many Scandinavians served in the Roman legions as auxiliaries. Warrior graves filled with weapons and luxury goods from this area suggest that early Scandinavian society was increasingly dominated by a warrior elite. This warrior elite served through the *comitatus*, a group headed by a warlord who amassed wealth through plunder and doled out its portions to his armed retainers. These warrior bands competed for the wealth spurred by contact with Rome (Haywood, pp. 19-20, 24).

While the western Roman Empire fell to the advance of wandering Germanic tribes from the continent, the Scandinavian peoples fortified their villages. They began a very gradual process of developing kingdoms, such as the one around the pagan cult site of Uppsala. Many of these kingdoms were established by the eighth century CE (Haywood, p. 20-21). Also by the eight century CE, Western Europe had stabilized somewhat from its post-Roman collapse: trade between Scandinavia and the Continent resumed (Haywood, p. 10).

Two other phenomena were present by the eighth century. The Scandinavians seemed to have developed considerable advances in shipbuilding technology, opening the far seas to them. At the same time, Scandinavian lands were suffering from overpopulation demanding relief (Haywood, pp. 9-10). Thus, the stage was set for the Viking era.

The Vikings

The term *i viking* means "to plunder." Thus, properly speaking, the Vikings were only those Scandinavians who went on raids. Most Scandinavians remained behind as peaceful farmers. But it is the raiders who made the colorful histories that fascinate us (Haywood, pp. 8-9, 46).

The Viking Age begins in Anglo-Saxon England. In the year 789 CE an incident with Scandinavian raiders led to the death of a local English official called a reeve. Later in 793 CE, the monastery at Lindisfarne was infamously raided, much to the horror of Christian Europe (Haywood, pp. 50-51).

What started the Viking Age? It has been suggested the Vikings were aware of forced conversions of Heathens on the Continent from Charles the Great, also known as Charlemagne (Ferguson, pp. 51-53). The raid at Lindisfarne has thus sometimes been construed in religious terms, an act of revenge by Heathens against Christians (Ferguson, p. 54). More likely, however, the raiders wanted what Germanic raiders had wanted for centuries: loot. Monasteries acted as repositories of poorly guarded valuables and relics, and were a tempting target. With such wealth an individual Viking could amass a personal fortune and settle down later; others might use it to finance political ambitions back home (Haywood, pp. 8-9, 11).

The story of the Vikings is too unwieldy to relay here in any great depth. But a very brief overview might suggest the incredibly broad range of their activities.

Vikings raids intensified on Anglo-Saxon England. In time the Vikings came not just to raid, but to settle. Many Anglo-Saxon kingdoms fell to the Great Heathen Army and became what was known as the Danelaw, centered on the city of York to the north. It took some effort for the kingdom of Wessex to reclaim those lost lands (Haywood, p. 62). At this time the Vikings also established a settlement in Ireland at Dublin (Haywood, p. 72).

On the Continent, Vikings spread out in all directions. They raided France, eventually occupying Normandy (Haywood, p. 81). Viking raids into Muslim controlled territory around Spain were eventually rebuffed (Haywood, pp. 58-59). To the East, Vikings established the proto-Russian states of Novgorod and Kiev (Haywood, pp. 102-103).

Vikings made it to Greenland (Haywood, p. 96). Literary and archeological evidence confirms they made it to North America long before Columbus, though they didn't stay permanently (Haywood, pp. 98).

There were two somewhat related trends that ended the Viking Age. One was, in so many words, "modernity." With all the fighting men seeking power and wealth, eventually one would predominate among the others. As local warlords fell to the onslaught of would-be monarchs, kingdoms were established. Centralized monarchies soon discovered that taxation of subjects was a more reliable method than raids for amassing wealth, and that ordered peace was generally preferable to incessant war. The Viking chiefdoms soon dissolved as medieval Scandinavian kingdoms emerged (Haywood, p. 11).

The other was Christianity (Haywood, pp. 115-116). Missionaries from continental European and Anglo-Saxon England had been penetrating Scandinavia for some time. While they were often met with fierce opposition, eventually Christianity triumphed through coercion by the state. The would-be monarchs among the Vikings found that Christianity suited their interests. They could extract a cut in financing Christian infrastructure, i.e.., building churches and such. They could rely on a literate clerical order as advisors. Those same clergy could promote their divine right to rule

The Christian missionary-king Olaf Tryggvason confronts the statue of Thor in a temple, as envisioned by the artist Halfdan Egedius. Snorre Sturluson, *Kongesagaer* (1899)

(Heather, p. 569). Finally, Christianity replaced the manifold morass of many local cults of polytheism with a religion that was theoretically unitary in scope and power, thus reinforcing a centralized state (Heather, pp. 571-572; Haywood, pp. 116).

With new monarchies who survived on taxation rather than plunder, and with a new religion that paid lip service to peace and the brotherhood of Christian nations, the Viking Age drew to a close.

Iceland

Iceland was discovered in the 860s CE, and settlement began in the 870s. By 930 CE all the decent farming land had been claimed (Haywood, pp. 92). Aside from relieving general overpopulation in the Scandinavian countries, another impetus for colonization was political. As King Harold Finehair consolidated his power in becoming the first king of a united Norway, many fled his rule. DNA studies suggest the majority of women of Iceland have Celtic ancestry, and were concubines or slaves taken by male Viking raiders (Ferguson, pp. 163-164).

As a reaction to the centralized monarchy they fled, the Icelandic settlers developed a different government. A body called the *Althing*, embodying judicial and legislative powers, was established to govern, but it held no executive body to enforce its decisions. A *Lawspeaker* was the nominal head of this body. Regional assemblies called *things* were set up as well. At the local level, local officials called *godar* (singular: *godi*) who held both secular and religious functions, advocated for their clients (Ferguson, pp. 165-166).

Icelandic society was very legalistic (Ferguson, pp. 167), though they shared a different notion of the law than we moderns. The *godar* advocated for their clients within the regional *things* and the *Althing*. If warrior prowess served Vikings in other countries, facility with litigation could win an Icelandic man renown. For severe crimes a man could be sentenced to *outlawry*, meaning he no longer held any rights within society and could be hunted down as an animal (Byock, pp. 225-226). However, as the *Althing* lacked any kind of police force or army to enforce its decisions, it was left to the citizenry at large to punish outlaws (Ferguson, p. 173).

As the rest of the Scandinavian countries fell to monarchy and Christianization, Iceland soon found itself in a precarious predicament. Christian missionaries had made inroads into Iceland, and a sizeable portion of the population was now Christian. Heathens and Christians found it difficult to live under the same law, and civil war seemed imminent. Further, external forces were bearing down on Iceland. Christian Europe was threatening an economic boycott of Iceland unless the island converted. The King of Norway was harassing Icelandic citizens in his country, and a Norwegian invasion seemed plausible (Ferguson, pp. 303-306).

Being a legalistic society, a legal solution was sought. The Lawspeaker of the *Althing* was tasked to decide an outcome. One fateful night he went into trance. When he came to, he offered the following solution. Outwardly the island would be Christian as its official religion. Inwardly, what religion a family practiced was not a concern of the state, as long as it did not offer public sacrifice to the gods (Ferguson, pp. 304-306).

This so-called compromise spared Iceland from immediate civil war, as well as economic strangulation from Christian Europe. Some say that it allowed the myths of the Heathen gods to survive underground, rather than being totally wiped out as they were on the Continent or in England.

Inside and Outside

In the Roman era, on the continent, Tacitus tells us the gods were honored in sacred groves. Archaeology also confirms the presence of votive deposits and sacrifices in bogs. Groves and bogs—the early Germans were given to honoring the deities in natural settings.

While Heathens never completely lost their reverence for natural landscapes, in the age of the *comitatus*, it is presumed the gods started coming inside. Perhaps this began with Odin, the patron of aristocratic warlords who feasted their retainers in their halls. The Anglo-Saxons had built enough sturdy temples that Christians could easily convert them to churches (Turville-Petre, p. 237). By Scandinavian times, Heathens used a *vé* (sanctuary) or a *hof* (temple) (Turville-Petre, pp. 238-240).

We saw in *Eyrbyggja Saga* that Thorolf built a temple to his god, Thor. But the surrounding natural area was considered so sacred that no one could relieve themselves on it. Thor was after all a god of the fertility of the fields, the deity whose rains and lightning hallowed the crops. In the Scandinavian era Thor had temple cults, but place names indicate he was also connected to mounds, rocks and islands (Turville-Petre, p. 94).

Thor Cults

Iceland especially honored Thor. Many place names there attest to his popularity. So, too, do personal names—a quarter of the original settlers in Iceland seem to have personal names derived from Thor. Anyone who reads Icelandic Sagas can become easily confused by an endless list of Thorgrims, Thorbergs, Thorolfs and the like. A practice was known whereby a child was dedicated to Thor, thus taking on a theophoric name as a sign of devotion. Thor was considered the god of the pillars which upheld the house (Turville-Petre, pp. 86-88).

Among the Scandinavian mainland, Thor was certainly known, especially in Norway. He is the god first mentioned when ritual sacrifice is given, and was the chief deity at the temples of Trondheim and *Guthbrand i Dolum* (Turville-Petre, pp. 90-91). In Sweden at the temple of Uppsala, he is one of three gods given cultic statues, along with Wodan (Odin) and Fricco (Freyr). The Swedes seemed to emphasize his fertility aspects. In Denmark there are a variety of topographical names with the Thor element (Turville-Petre, pp. 93-94).

The Hammer and the Cross

The Thor's Hammer is often worn by modern Heathens as their default symbol. This references its use in historical times when it became increasingly widespread among Heathens as Christianity penetrated; the hammers served as symbols and probably as protective amulets as well (Turville-Petre, pp. 83, 89). At first Heathens did not see Christianity as a threat, seeing Christ as just another god among many. Gradually, though, the Christian intent to dominate and eradicate became clear. Thor was the god of the commoners and traditionalists who clung to their folkways. The Red Thor was opposed to the White Christ, as it were. Thor was the guardian of the gods and the people against an alien threat (Turville-Petre, p. 89).

That Thor was the defender of Heathendom against Christianity evolved naturally from his status as defender of order and rightness. The Lore, as we have seen, spoke of his many exploits fighting giants and monsters. Skalds praised his deeds, celebrating the gory details by which Thor bashed in the heads of his enemies and made them bleed (Turville-Petre, pp. 85-86).

Bronze statuette of Thor holding his Hammer (sculpted as an extension of his beard). Eyrarland, Iceland; Viking Age. National Museum of Iceland. Photo by L3u, Wikimedia Commons, CC BY-SA 3.0.

Chapter Eight: Runes and the Swastika

Runes

The runes were developed on the Continent sometime in the first two centuries CE, probably as a result of contact with the literate Romans and their Latin alphabet (Pollington, *Runes*, pp. 79, 89). Runes were used as a writing system to scratch or carve angular symbols on hard surfaces like wood, stone or bone (Pollington, *Runes*, pp. 31-32). While this writing system largely had prosaic purposes, nonetheless there were esoteric uses of runes (Pollington, *Runes*, p. 296), much of which still confuses modern scholars and is hotly debated (Pollington, *Runes*, p. 23; Macleod and Mees, p. 1).

Under the influence of Christianity runes were also written with ink on parchment, especially by bored Christian monks with antiquarian interests (Pollington, *Runes*, p. 57).

Two or more runes could be combined into something called a *bind-rune*. This may have developed simply as a way of saving space, but may also have contained an esoteric understanding to it (Pollington, *Runes*, p. 101).

Lore makes Odin the god who discovered the runes (Hollander, p. 36), and Heimdall the god who taught the runes to humanity (or at least to the nobility) (Hollander, p. 127).

The Nordendorf Fibula

One interesting archaeological find from the later continental period is an artefact known as the Nordendorf Fibula, a fibula being a brooch or pin for fashioning garments. It was found in what is now Bavaria, Germany, and is dated to the mid-500s CE (McKinnel and Simek, p. 48).

The artefact contains a runic inscription. The inscription invokes three deities: *Logathore, Wodan* and *Wigi-Thonar. Logathore* is difficult to translate, but may refer to Loki. *Wodan* is the earlier name for Odin. Wigi-Thonar seems to refer to a "battle Thor" or "hallowing Thor" (Pollington, *Runes*, pp. 199-200; McKinnel and Simek, pp. 48-49; Macleod and Mees, pp. 17-18).

The nature of the runic amulet and its message is disputed. It might be a Christian artefact, warning that the Heathen gods are evil seducers, or it might be a Heathen artefact intoning a blessing of some sort (Pollington, *Runes*, p. 302; McKinnel and Simek, p. 49). Others have interpreted it as a love charm (Macleod and Mees, p. 19).

Regardless, it shows that people in the mid sixth century of the south of Germany still believed in Heathen gods on some level. It also shows that the deity we know as Thor was among them, and presumably an important one if he is one of three named deities.

Runes in Viking Age Scandinavia

In the Viking age the only god mentioned by runes is Thor (Macleod and Mees, pp. 29-30). "May Thor hallow these runes" or some variant thereof is a phrase that appears on the Velanda runestone from Sweden, and the Glavendrup stone and the Sonder Kirkeby runestone from Denmark (Turville-Petre, pp. 82-83; Pollington, *Runes*, pp. 299-302).

The Korpabron runestone from Södermanland in Sweden bears a coded rune inscription which is usually translated as "may Thor safeguard." The Virring Stone reads: **tur viki þisi kuml**, "may Thor hallow this memorial." (Turville-Petre, p. 83)

In these instances above, we can see the runecarvers call on Thor to bless and to ward. Thor empowers the runic carvings, and in one instance at least is directly asked to hallow a memorial. We might recall from the Lore section the episode at Balder's funeral pyre where Thor raised his hammer to hallow the fires.

Memorial runestone from Stenkvista, Sweden, showing Thor's Hammer. Image courtesy of the Swedish National Heritage Board (*Riksantikvarieämbetet*), Public Domain.

Runes in Medieval Iceland

In Iceland at the medieval era, bindrunes came to be heavily stylized and used as sigils in magical spells (Pollington, *Runes*, p. 290). These were called *galdrastafir* (Flowers, p.15). *Galdrastafir* are

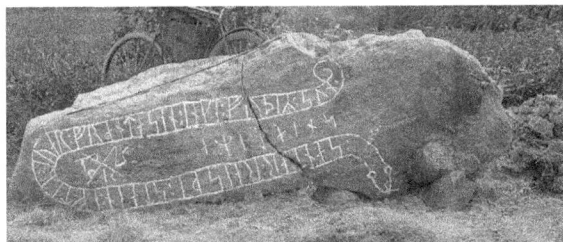

Memorial runestone from Korpabronn, Sweden. At left, inside the rune ribbon, the X-shaped figure is a bindrune that is thought to mean "may Thor safeguard." Image courtesy of the Swedish National Heritage Board (*Riksantikvarieämbetet*), Public Domain.

found in a medieval spell book, a *grimoire,* called the *Galdrabók*, which was written by several authors from the 16th and 17th centuries (Flowers, pp. 29-30) These spells exist in some twilight world between Christianity and paganism, incorporating elements of both (Flowers, p. 38). The spells call on old Heathen deities as well as deities of the classical world, and entities that Christians would call demons or fallen angels. The *galdrastafir* reveal an essentially *magical worldview* rather than a religious one. The magician was concerned not with a coherent or moral theology, but with the efficacy of the spells he cast.

An example of one of these is the so-called "charm to make a woman silent." Thor is called on along with other Heathen gods, and Christian devils, to prevent a woman from speaking. A *galdrastafr* is to be placed in the woman's drink, and the spell intoned (Flowers, p. 77-78).

The mighty Thor had fallen far indeed. The champion of Heathenry against the forces of chaos and against Christianity was now just another ingredient in a magical roofie from a (misogynist?) male magician. Nonetheless it shows that Thor was still remembered and called upon in some capacity. In fact, Thor is mentioned only behind Odin in the list of Heathen beings whom the spells invoke (Flowers, p. 39).

Runes in Bergen, Norway

The runes survived in Norway, too, though in a much-simplified form that became considerably widespread among the population.

Bergen was founded on the west coast of Norway. It became a center of trade and even served as Norway's capital for a time. A plethora of rune-inscribed objects have been found from Bergen's medieval era (Pollington, *Runes*, p. 215). These are often inscribed on small pieces of wood, and thus have been called the Bergen runesticks (Macleod and Mees, p. 30). One such runestick proclaims:

Hail to you, and be in good spirits!
May Thor receive you,
And Odin own you! (Macleod and Mees, p. 30)

ᚦᛆᚱ ᚦᛁᚴ ᚦᛁᚴ ᚠᛁ᚜ᛒᛁᛚ ᚦᚼ ᛏᛁᛠᛁ

This missive was written in *galdralag*, or incantation meter. Possibly
then it has a magical purpose, though we cannot be sure. It has been interpreted variously as a simple expression of good luck, or a funerary charm
for a corpse (Macleod and Mees, p. 30). Whatever it was, it is significant
that Thor is called alongside the chieftain of the gods to invoke whatever
sentiment the rune carver sought.

The Swastika

It is hard to think of symbol given to more of a Pavlovian reaction than
the swastika; the very sight of it is linked to the horrors of National Social-
ism. And yet, the Nazis didn't invent the swastika.

The swastika is found on ancient relics all over the Indo-European
world, from pagan altars in northern En-
gland to temples in India. The swastika
first appears in Sanskrit as *svastika,* and
appears to be associated with good luck
and well-being (*Encyclopedia Brittanica*).
At some point, this crooked cross symbol
becomes associated with the solar wheel,
and thus the sky, and thus with sky gods.
The swastika seems to have become associated with the sunwheel, and fire (Davidson, p. 83).

The swastika has been used by various Germanic peoples throughout history
(Macleod and Mees, p. 100). Swastikas
are commonly spotted on surviving runic

Anglo-Saxon copper-alloy swastika
brooch, 6th-7th centuries. 51 mm.
Naburn, Yorkshire. Portable Antiquities Scheme, British Museum,
YORYM-285423. CC BY-SA 4.0.

charms (Macleod and Mees, p. 9), where the symbol seems to imbue the text with a sense of luck or holiness (Macleod and Mees, p. 21), and several runic inscriptions to Thor contain the swastika (Davidson, p. 83). In Anglo-Saxon times we find the swastika on a variety of funerary urns and disk brooches, suggesting it had funerary significance (Davidson, p. 83; Pollington, *The Elder Gods*, p. 200). We might recall that Thor was called on in Norse times to hallow runes and memorials; perhaps the swastika served the same purpose for the Anglo-Saxon dead. Meanwhile, Horagalles, the Saami god equivalent to Thor, is depicted with both hammers and swastika (Turville-Petre, p. 84).

It is clear the swastika was an ancient, wide spread symbol. It was associated with holiness, luck, and power. At times it seems to have been associated with the sun, or more broadly the sky. In the minds of some, these are qualities that linked the symbol to Thor.

I am not suggesting, as some have, Heathens and other Indo-European pagans should reclaim the swastika and restore it to its original meaning. As long as the horrors of the death camps are within living memory, and as long as Heathens and pagans are an ineffectual minority in the modern West, the quest to reclaim the swastika from its Nazi appropriation seems quixotic. But in the interests of truth we should be aware of its origins and its historic uses.

Detail of the Virring stone, reading **þur uiki þisi kuml**. In normalized Old Norse this is *Þórr vigi þessi kuml*, "May Thor hallow this monument." Thorsen, *De Danske Runemindesmærker*, 1879

Summary of History

We see the first stirrings of Thor as the proto-Indo-European "striker god," a deity with a weapon who fights chaos monsters, and a deity of oak and lightning who also givers fertility. The PIE language gives birth to many descendant languages. PIE religion likewise bestows its theology and various mythological motifs to its descendants. As the proto-Indo-Europeans spread, they develop into varying offshoots. Germanic languages begin to develop, and it is through linguistic criteria (as opposed to some anachronistic racialist agenda) that we can begin to define Germanic peoples and religion.

The Germans on the Continent know a Donar, who is likened either to Hercules (because he is a hero-god who uses a distinct weapon) or to Jupiter (because he is a sky god who wields a lightning bolt). The Germanic tribes allegedly sung cultic songs to him before battle, and he is worshipped (along with other deities) in sacred groves. Oaks particularly are sacred to him. He is appeased with standard animal sacrifice (as opposed to the human sacrifice of Mercury/Odin). He is often mentioned in everything from runes to baptism vows alongside Odin.

The Anglo-Saxons knew a god Thunor, or Thunderer. A day of the week was named after him and various place name in England have a "thunder" component. Presumably he was an important deity. However, the scant Anglo-Saxon record does not afford us much definitive proof of his cult. That swastikas are found on funerary urns may suggest Thunor had a role in hallowing gravesides, but the evidence is inconclusive.

Thor is one of the principal deities of Scandinavia and the Viking Age. He is entreated both as a god who gives fertility to the fields as well as the god who defends against chaos. He has temple cults in Scandinavia, and in Iceland the household pillars are dedicated to him. He becomes the defender of Heathenry in its later stages against encroaching Christianity. Despite Odin and Heimdall being linked with runes in the surviving Lore, the runic artefacts of this era call on Thor as their god.

This runic link continues into Medieval times as well. A magician's spell in Iceland invokes Thor alongside other Heathen gods, as well as denizens of the Christian hell. An artefact from Bergen, Norway, invoked Thor alongside Odin (for a purpose we do not completely understand). Before the Swastika suffered the indignity of being associated with totalitarianism and genocide, it was a holy symbol that was at times connected with Thor.

Thor was clearly a well-known, well-loved deity in all epochs of Heathen experience. He was a god who could protect and champion, give luck and fertility, and bless and empower.

Silver filigree Thor's Hammer amulets from Skåne (left) and Bredsattra (right), Sweden. Swedish Historical Museum, CC BY 2.5.

Chapter Nine: Urglaawe

This section was a late addition to the book. Of all the various Heathen traditions, I am least familiar with Urglaawe. However, its exclusion from this book would have been an oversight.

I am indebted to Robert L. Schreiwer for furnishing material and proof-reading this section.

Urglaawe

The Continental Heathens were Christianized during their interactions with the Roman Empire, sometimes by choice and often by coercion. They left us no primary texts written by their own hands; what we know of them comes from outside observers and archaeological artefacts (see the chapter in this book on Continental Heathenry). However, remnants of Heathen traditions survived in folklore. One can, for instance, see faint echoes of pre-Christian sentiments in some of the many fairy tales collected by the brothers Grimm.

A vein of folklore traditions resides in the Germanic settlers of the New World. As the High German word for German is *deutsch*, this became mistranslated in the American colonies as "Dutch." And as many of these settlers initially concentrated in the colony of Penn's Woods, these people came to be known as the Pennsylvania Dutch. Today this group of people is more properly referred to as the *Deitsch*, named after the dialect of German that they spoke (and that many of their descendants still speak as a first language) (Schreiwer and Eckhart, p. viii).

The Thirty Years War had devastated parts of central Europe. Fleeing the poverty and religious turmoil of the era, Germanic speaking settlers left in droves to America for a better life (Schreiwer, pp. 3-4). The *Deitsch* are typically considered those Germanic peoples who had emigrated from the late 17th century through the early 19th century—and their modern day descendants (Schreiwer and Eckhart, p. 12).

"Urglaawe" is a neologism which means "primal faith" in *Deitsch*. It is the section of Heathenry that concentrates on the folklore and folk practices of those Germanic settlers. Continental and Scandinavian Heathen sources are used for supplemental information (Schreiwer and Eckhart, p. viii).

Urglaawe is connected with two mystical practices among the *Deitsch* (Schreiwer and Eckhart, 2012, p. ix). *Braucherei*, referred to in English as "powwowing," is a healing practice. While overtly Christian, there resides within itself a deeper layer of pre-Christian belief (Schreiwer and Eckhart, pp. 9-10). *Hexerei*, meanwhile, is a related mystical practice that can be loosely described as witchcraft. Hexerei differentiates itself from Braucherei in not being tied exclusively to healing (Schreiwer and Eckhart, pp. 35-36).

Urglaawe shares many of the same deities as Norse Heathenry, but also contains a few other deities not found elsewhere. Chief among these is Frau Holle (Schreiwer and Eckhart, p. ix). She is a magical deity thought to preside over cycles of life, and is in many ways the matron of the tradition (Schreiwer and Eckhart, pp. 40-41). Holle is thought to have guided the Deitsch immigration to America (Schreiwer, p. 4).

Dunner

Within Urglaawe, Thor's equivalent is Dunner. He is the exponent of thunder, lightening and rain. He is the god for the common folk. He lends his name to the *Deitsch* word for Thursday, *Dunnerschdaag*. Oak trees are sacred to him (Schreiwer and Eckhart, pp. 14-15).

There are some particular folk practices regarding Dunner related to the agricultural lifestyle of the early *Deitsch*. Thursday was an auspicious day; on that day cattle were first put out to pasture, and it was one of the most popular days for weddings (Schreiwer and Eckhart, p. 15).

Dunner was considered the protector of beasts of burdens, especially goats. Red is considered his sacred color, and flora and fauna that contain red are thought to be under his protection (Schreiwer and Eckhart, pp. 14-15).

We find Dunner performing the same essential hallowing and warding functions as Thor. The color red was used as a charm, such as red underwear being worn to ward off rheumatism. Rounded stones were set atop fence posts to imitate the thunderbolt, and thus invoke the god's protection of cattle (Schreiwer and Eckhart, p. 15). Finally, every May, Dunner is thought to win in battle against three frost giants known as *Reifres*, symbolizing the triumph of spring over winter (Schreiwer and Eckhart, pp. 14, 51)

The Deitsch—many of whom were raised Mennonite or Amish—can find a Heathen echo in their folk practices. Dunner lives somewhere within that tradition, watching over the folk as he always does. Somewhere, deep behind the Cross, one can find the Hammer.

Thor as envisioned by artist J. C. Dollman.
Guerber, *Myths of the Norsemen* (1919)

PART III: MODERN EXPERIENCE

The reader, having completed the previous parts on lore and history, now knows generally how Thor was seen by his followers, and where and when he was honored. As the bard said, "what is past is prologue" (*The Tempest*, Act 2, scene 1).

In the next section, I present *my* experiences with Thor, my own individual interpretation of him as derived from private reflection and mystical experiences. I discuss how I see him, as an individual of the modern West. A term commonly used in Heathenry for approaching a deity from this angle is *UPG—unverified personal gnosis*. It serves to emphasize that UPG is exactly that—both personal and unverified.

I present these views and experiences for two reasons. First, for those who don't have their own UPG, this may give them a starting point with which to conduct their own explorations. Second, for those who do have their own UPG, this gives them something against which they may contrast and compare their own experiences. In either case, UPG fosters a dialogue about Thor as an objective, independent, spiritual being, still operating in the modern world with his own personality and agenda, even a thousand years after the Viking Age and its Lore.

I also present suggested rites that fellow moderns may use to approach him. These rituals are designed for slightly different audiences in mind: At the end of the day one needs to take their religion out of the book and into modern experience. The reader is invited to keep what works for them and discard the rest.

The section will close with a guest essay, a perspective different from my own. Laura "Snow" Fuller is many things: a fellow Heathen, a colleague on the Troth board of directors, a drinking buddy, and—not least—my beloved wife. But most salient for this work, she happens to be a woman, a woman's studies major, and a feminist. It is sometimes said that Heathenry suffers from a paucity of female voices, and all too often the religion is held captive to a chorus of macho male Viking wanna-bes. I felt that a woman's perspective on Thor was a necessary supplement to this work.

Thor as envisioned by modern author and artist Diana L. Paxson.
Used by permission.

Chapter Ten: Unverified Personal Gnosis

One should be cautiously respectful when listening to someone else proffer their UPG, until one has a reason not to. I say *respectful* because someone's experience is **their** experience, and should not be automatically condemned simply because it is not one's own experience or viewpoint. I say *cautiously*, however, because admittedly under the banner of UPG there are those who have advocated some very bizarre claims, dangerous practices, or obnoxious forms of self-aggrandizement. It's a fine line to tread: wanting to be open minded without giving credence to every unsubstantiated claim.

In the great debate between whether Lore or UPG is more valid, I have taken a middle ground that incorporates both paradigms as useful tools that can reinforce one another. Lore is, to my mind, a boundary of sorts that anchors our notions of the deities to a historical, culturally enshrined reality. UPG that does not contradict Lore, that does not tarry too far beyond those boundaries, should be given a fair consideration. UPG can elucidate strands of a deity not revealed by Lore, or can supplement them for a modern reality. Both can be different sources of light illuminating the same subject.

With that in mind, the following is my UPG on Thor. These insights are gleaned from private trance sessions and meditations.

Personality

Thor is usually portrayed in Lore with a hard edge, implacable in battle and with a temper often on a short leash. I firmly believe that is an aspect of his personality, but must be taken into context. Thor is usually portrayed in Lore in antagonistic situations: fighting giants, trading barbs with his father, Odin, or dealing with Loki's machinations. (If it were my job to clean up Loki's messes, I probably wouldn't always be in the best humor, either.)

When not in a situation that calls for combat or argument, Thor otherwise seems even-tempered and good natured. In the tale where Thjalfi lamed his goat and became enraged, the pleas of Thjalfi's father for mercy did mollify the god, and Thor showed the family mercy. Thor comes across to me as essentially fair and even tempered. He desires what is best for his followers, and wishes them happiness and a good life.

He does of course demand a certain base moral code as he understands it—one based on hospitality, fair play, loyalty and reciprocity. And he demands that his followers have the strength and diligence to be honorable folk. But he is otherwise not interested in proscribing a detailed moral code to his adherents, nor does he foster a particularly complicated theology or philosophy.

Simple, yet strong and powerful. Kind when he can be, ferocious when he must be. Assuming a broad core of ethical behavior but not particularly interested in micromanaging morality. All of these notions describe him well.

Intelligence

Thor does not exactly enjoy a reputation for being intellectual. There is a perception among many that he is a strong brute employed best when bashing giants with his hammer, fit for little else. To this I would say there is a certain economy in Thor's style. Sometimes the simplest method to resolve a situation is not through involved strategy or arcane magic, but direct force.

The story of Alvis the dwarf does illustrate that Thor is capable of confronting an intellectual foe. He does this not by outwitting his foes, but by letting them outwit themselves. He gave Alvis just enough rope for the dwarf to hang himself. The pompous fool seemed all too eager to spout off his knowledge of Lore, completely oblivious to the imminent danger of the rising sun. Thor demonstrated not intellectual prowess in the academic sense, but skill in assessing the lay of the terrain and exploiting his foe's personality flaws.

I would suggest there are different dimensions of intelligence. Strategy in the broadest sense, the "big picture" as it were, falls to Odin. Odin sees the end goal and marshals his forces from point A to point B and then to point C, as if on a grand chess board. Thor sees not the end goal but the immediate terrain before him, and knows best how to deal with it, often by force and sometimes by chicanery.

In my private sessions with deities, some (like Odin) are apt to wax eloquent on broad topics: the meaning of Ragnarok, the nature of the human condition, the ultimate goals of one's life, etc. Thor is more apt to offer practical advice to counter an immediate threat or remedy a pressing conundrum. For that reason, he is extremely useful to cultivate as an ally.

Loki

Laufeyson can be a controversial figure, at least within American Heathenry (the situation seems to differ in Europe). There is a debate as to whether or not Loki is really a deity, whether or not he should be included in public ritual, and to what degree the surviving Lore paints a fair representation of him and his role in Ragnarok. It is not my intent to replicate all the details of said argument here. My question is: given the perceived controversy, how does Thor relate to Loki?

The Lore paints Loki as Thor's travelling companion, and the two were together at Thor's most famous adventure when he was beguiled by the trials of Utgarda-Loki. For that reason, some presume an amicable relationship between the two, and are wont to hail them together.

In my experience, Thor has a more complicated relationship with Laufeyson. As can be seen from *Lokasenna*, Thor's threats to bash Loki are ultimately the only thing that evicts Laufeyson from the setting.

In private workings, Thor seems to take a nuanced stance to Loki. Thor recognizes Loki brings certain talents to the table, and that Loki appeals to a certain type of individual who may benefit from Loki's ministrations. But much like a controlled fire has the potential to wreak havoc if left unchecked, Thor casts an ever-suspicious eye on Loki. Loki eschews boundaries, and boundaries (particularly against chaos) are needed if both Midgard and Asgard are to prosper.

Thor's viewpoint (*as expressed to me*) seems to be that whatever role Loki has to play, it is a role played on the outskirts of the community, not within. The son of Odin does not seem keen on being hailed alongside Odin's blood-brother within a communal, public ritual.

Offerings

This may seem like a trivial section. But if our religion is about gifting, then the gifts we give are of utmost importance.

It seems shared UPG among Heathens that Thor enjoys strong drink (*Our Troth*, vol. 1, p. 237). Mead, beer (especially darker ales such as stouts and porters), whiskey and coffee have all been offerings that he seems to appreciate. He also enjoys meats and cheeses; at rituals I have thrown raw steak or raw pork on the bonfire, to good effect. As a god associated with the harvest, especially at Loafmass, the first fruits of one's garden would be appropriate. Chocolate was not known to the Old World, but in this modern era he does not seem to eschew it.

He may be honored with athletic competitions and mock battles. He likes strong incense as well—musky, or indicative of the forest or rain. Finally, while not one of the Vanir, he by no means eschews sexual relations among consenting adults. I throw the last sentence in because Thor is at home among the crowd, among the common people assembled to have a good time. He seems to enjoy a good party with all its hallmarks—food, drink, play and sex.

Thor, or a figure inspired by the iconography of Thor, carved on a baptismal font from Ottrava, Götland, Sweden. Stephens, *Thunor the Thunderer* (1878)

Chapter Eleven: Cult of Thor

With the previous considerations in mind, I would like to relay the UPG results of a special trance session. These are considerations of what Thor wants regarding a cult. I here use the term "cult" in the Roman sense of the word (*cultus*), which are the observances, theologies and material artefacts related to a particular deity.

Thor bid me to consider his cult throughout the various historical eras. What did Donar mean to Continental tribes? Who was Thunor to the Anglo-Saxons? And how did the Icelandic people perceive Thor? What emerged then was a broad picture of this deity. To that picture he supplemented some ideas that upgraded his cult for a modern era.

Four general pillars of a cult were relayed: *Protection, Hallowing, Fertility,* and *Rightness*. Each will be scrutinized in detail below.

Protection

Perhaps the best-known aspect of Thor from the Lore is his penchant to engage in combat with various beings who are inimical to the gods. Usually he does this simply by utilizing his hammer, Mjolnir, against whom none can stand. In at least two instance though, regarding the dwarf Alvis, and in *The Saga of Egil and Asmund*, Thor was able to outwit his foe.

Thor feels if an individual has nothing worth fighting for, they effectively have nothing worth living for. Thor noted that he has many soldiers, active or former, within his ranks of followers. The concept of protection, however, is far broader than a merely martial concept.

Thor asks his followers to become protectors themselves, though he leaves the exact details to individuals. Every individual needs to find something they hold dear, something worthy of blood, tears and sweat. For many people that's a family and home. For others it may well be a local community, a kindred, a national organization or a country. Thor, son of the Earth, also invites us to consider the "web of nature" (ecosphere) as worthy of protection.

Whatever the cause, once an individual has chosen, they must actively guard it with strength and wit, knowing that defense may entail sacrifice in the process.

Hallowing

Because of his defensive attributes, Thor is usually invoked in modern Heathen rituals as a hallowing deity. This is often accomplished by some version of a Hammer rite within Scandinavian-derived traditions. However, in Anglo-Saxon Heathenry, Thor (Thunor) is often invoked while ambulating around the ritual area with sacred fire.

Both of these scenarios work. The hammer, the bane of giants and a symbol of might and mane, when uplifted serves as a banishing symbol. Fire, meanwhile, burns away pests and germs, and keeps wild animals at bay.

Thor, the protector of man, revels in his status as a hallowing deity. He invites us to consider encircling our inner-yard with hammer or fire to keep the forces of the outer-yard at bay.

Fertility

In Heathenry, the go-to for fertility is usually one of the Vanir, especially Ing-Frey. Thor does, however, convey a measure of fertility to his followers. The Anglo-Saxon Rune Poem verse for *āc*, or oak, speaks of acorns feeding animals. Likewise, the hallowing aspects of Thor kept the fields safe, ensuring harvest. It was in this latter aspect, no doubt, that throngs of peasants hailed the Thunderer, elevating him to the most popular deity of the Viking era in Iceland.

The fertility of Thor comes with a price—he will not help those who will not help themselves. He expects those not afflicted with mental or physical handicaps to hold down gainful employment and be productive members of their family, tribe and community. In the modern age, fertility means less about tilling the fields and more about hard work at whatever vocation one finds oneself.

Rightness

Like most pre-Christian deities, Thor does not proscribe a long list of morals to his adherents. He does expect a certain ethical direction in one's life, however.

Thor stands for hospitality, common decency, fair play and honesty. He upholds the path of everyday morality, an honest day's work without exploitation of the weak or bamboozling one's neighbors. He does not abide those who flaunt communal law for their own gain.

Other Considerations

In addition to the four pillars mentioned above, there are other hallmarks of a Thor cult.

Health: Thor generally espouses a life of strength and the physicality to back it up. One needs strength to protect; one needs to be wholesome to hallow. Weightlifting and other strength training activities are very fitting pastimes to honor the god.

Oaks: Oaks have always been sacred to Thor, and in the earliest epochs he was honored in sacred groves. While planting sacred groves is beyond the wherewithal of most of us, Thor desires worship outside where possible. Parks and forests with oak trees should be especially sought.

Magic: Thor is the only god mentioned in the surviving runic artefacts of the Viking era; he was called on to hallow the runic inscription. This might be seen by modern esoteric workers, that Thor can hallow and empower their workings.

A word of caution, however; if Rightness is a path of his cult, then one's esoteric workings with Thor should be for the greater good or for defense. Invoking him to curse a rival at work to gain a promotion, or asking an oak tree to fall on your ex after a break-up, will probably not get you anywhere. We might remember one of the Medieval Icelandic spells did call on him "to shut up a woman," but in my experience, you get more traction with Thor when you ask him to help in loftier goals.

Thor has said that the power of the thunderstorm is a mystery that can be explored for his cult. Consider that the thunderstorm embodies all four pillars: its lightning *protects* and *hallows* by striking enemies, its rains grant *fertility* to drenched fields, and its *rightness* in the natural order of things is underscored by the idiom "as right as rain." In my section on liturgy, I give a Two Powers Meditation that invokes the powers of the thunderstorm.

Weaving It All Together

This section has focused on Thor as I know him, and what he desires from his followers as was relayed to me through UPG.

Whereas Odin may be capricious, Loki may be chaotic, and the Vanir can be mysterious, Thor is as rather straightforward as it gets for a Norse deity. And yet Thor is neither a simpleton nor a brute. He is possessed of great practical intelligence. His main focus is not force *per se* but hallowing and protection. That he has some esoteric side is demonstrated by the fact he was called upon by the runemasters.

Thor asks us to choose our causes, and once chosen, to abide by them. He upholds the common decency that ties people to their communities, and demands they have the strength and wherewithal to defend their own.

Thor is an essentially benevolent deity, though one terrifying to his enemies. He places few demands, and leverages those demands with rewards. He asks we live our lives with decency, honor and happiness.

Runestone showing Thor's face and Hammer. Åby, Södermanland, Sweden. Stephens, *Thunor the Thunderer* (1878)

Chapter Twelve: Rituals

This chapter will focus on liturgical methods to honor Thor. My audience will be Heathens, Druids, or general pagans/occultists. I have, at various times, been a member of all three communities, and this devotional has been written with all three in mind. Let me define my terms.

Heathen

Heathenry is usually defined as those who honor Germanic deities in a manner that is inspired by historic Germanic polytheism. Different Heathen groups vary in the degree to which they replicate known historical mechanics and understandings. Heathens largely honor *only* Germanic deities, at least within a specific rite. This sets them apart from more eclectic versions of Neopaganism, where it is not uncommon to see deities from different pantheons invoked in the same rite.

Heathens may also differ in cultural focus. The most widespread version is late Viking era Iceland, as that is the time and place that furnishes most of our information on Heathenry. Many such Heathens would identify with the label of "Ásatrú"—true to the Æsir, the tribe of gods of which Thor is a member. Others nominally in the Ásatrú camp may focus on other Scandinavian regions: Norway, Sweden or Denmark. Outside the Ásatrú camp are Heathens who internalize Anglo-Saxon England or old Continental Germanic forms of Heathenry. Meanwhile, those in the Urglaawe camp are inspired by the folklore of the Deitsch, or Pennsylvania-Germans.

In most sectors of Heathenry, the main point of any ritual is gifting the gods and ancestors, the "gift for a gift" theology we have already discussed. The focus therefore is *devotional*. The gods are entreated with gifts and in return, it is hoped, they provide their blessings.

In Heathenry, there are two basic forms of public ritual. A *blót* is the main type of ritual to honor a deity or spiritual being. A *blót,* properly speaking, involves a blood sacrifice, as was done in historical times. Nowadays most of us don't have the means (or perhaps even the inclination) to sacrifice animals; in most Heathen circles *blót* has come to informally mean any kind of votive rite. The other is a *sumbel*, which is several rounds of ritual toasting to gods and ancestors. *Blót* and *sumbel* were described vaguely by the historical sources, as discussed in the "Hakon the Good" summary of the Lore section in Part One.

Heathenry does have two culturally specific magical practices. The first are runes, which have been discussed elsewhere in this devotional. There is little evidence runes were historically used in divination, but in the modern era various "traditions" of runic divination have emerged and are now widespread. Runes can also be used for active magic; often they are intoned or sung, *galdered*. Rune-galder is typically attributed to Odin, but as was seen in the historical section, Thor was called on by runecarvers as well as Medieval magicians.

Aside from rune-galder, the other culturally specific magical tradition is *seidhr*. *Seidhr* is a poorly understood esoteric art, and how exactly it is defined depends largely on the individual studying it. It has been portrayed as everything from spinning magic to Viking battle magic. In the main it is generically a Norse form of witchcraft, where the mind/soul is manipulated to perform various acts that can affect people, animals, objects and nature (Sturluson, *Heimskringla*, p. 5). It also has an oracular (prophetic) component (Kunz, pp. 658-660). *Seidhr* is considered Freyja's art, but Odin did learn and master it.

While trance is not specifically mentioned in the sources, most modern imaginings of *seidhr* have trance as the foundational work. While trance can certainly be performed to Thor, he is not usually the recipient of *seidhr* work within Heathenry.

Druid

Druids, properly speaking, were the intelligentsia of the old Celtic tribes. According to Caesar, Druids studied for twenty years before they received such credentials (Caesar, pp. 334-339). There are Celtic polytheist Reconstructionists around these days; I am not sure if they have "Druids" or what those credentials entail if they do.

Regardless, I use "Druid" to connote a loosely related set of religions. In the last three centuries in the United Kingdom, as some people tired of both Christianity and the "progress" of the scientific-industrial order, new religions sprouted to offer people a third choice. These "Druid" groups imagined themselves as having ties to the Celtic past, but were founded on bad scholarship as well as pure invention. Regardless, they are now living traditions with their own validity. Druid groups vary widely, but most hold nature as sacred, and are open to various levels of occult experience (Carr-Gomm, "A Longer History of Druidry"). Many Druid groups, as you might imagine, lean toward all things Celtic, but some are more broadly based in cultural foci. In ADF, the Druid group with whom I have the most experience, it is not uncommon to find people pursuing some mix of Celtic and Germanic spirituality within a greater framework of nature reverence.

General Neopagan or Occult

Neopaganism encompasses many different spiritual paths. General Neopaganism is usually eclectic and occult-oriented, and often has at least a measure of nature reverence. There are certainly those individuals who may wish to honor Thor, and invoke him, and "work with him" (as the common parlance goes) without internalizing a specific spiritual label.

While other deities inside and outside the Norse pantheon might be closely connected to magic *per se*, as we have seen Thor was invoked in runic magic in the historical era. In the modern era he offers a vital service: warding and protection.

Liturgy

Liturgy is the collection of rites by which an individual or group conduct religious worship. It has been likened to following a script for a movie or play: there is a sequenced formula of instructions and "stage directions" that guide the individual or group in realizing a specific mood and plot. It is through liturgy that we and our fellow participants *experience* a religious reality.

In my view, liturgy can serve both or either of two broad categories: *devotional* or *magical.*

- Devotional rituals are designed to foster a mutually reciprocal relationship between the individual or group and the supernatural benefactor whom they are supplicating. The theological maxim of PIE religion and its descendants was *ghostis, "I give so that you may give," or as Heathens say, "a gift for a gift." The height of such rituals is an offering to the deity or spirit, with the expectation that said deity or spirit will be obligated to return a gift.
- Magical rituals, as one might expect, foster the esoteric. Magic is hard to define and notions of it vary widely. In general, two things must happen in regard to magic: 1) there is a change of con-

sciousness, allowing the participant(s) to perceive and perform in ways they could not otherwise, and 2) there is intent for a willed change, either in oneself or in the external universe.

These are broad categories, and in practice tend to coalesce in places. A ritual may include both devotional and magical workings. Some people feel that devotions to a deity empowers their magic, or that a magical act may itself be a devotion to a deity.

The Flow of Liturgical Energy

Rituals can be as simple or as complicated as participants desire or as the situation warrants. At one end of the spectrum, plenty of Heathens get by with simply cracking a beer open over a campfire and shouting a hearty "Hail Thor (or whatever deity)!" This is not exactly my idea of religion, especially if (as is usually the case) the alcohol used is cheap swill. At the other end of the spectrum I have heard of some Druidic rituals lasting up to three hours. To my mind this is overkill; any rite that takes more than an hour seems to strain the credulity and physicality of its participants.

Most of the **successful** rituals I have experienced incorporate a five-stage structure that delineates a dramatic flow of energy. These five stages might be likened to acts of Shakespeare's plays.

I: Introduction
II: Rising Action
III: Climax
IV: Falling Action
V: Conclusion

The flow of dramatic energy is introduced, built upon, reaches its crescendo, begins to dissipate, and then terminates in a satisfactory manner (Ray, "The Five-Act Play").

It has been said this five act dramatic structure lends itself well to religious ritual, and historically has operated within the Indo-European religious framework (Bonewits, pp. 23-24).

I. Introduction. The altar or ritual ground is prepared and purified. The participants assemble and are ritually purified. The presiding officiant welcomes the participants and formally states the purpose of said ritual.

75

II. *Rising Action.* The deities or spirits are invoked according to whatever mechanisms the spiritual traditions dictate.

III. *Climax.* Offerings are made to the deities or spirits in whatever proscribed manner. Usually the presiding officiant consecrates the offerings with a formal prayer.

IV. *Falling Action.* With the deities or spirits invited and placated, the participants can perform various workings in their name. These can be esoteric workings, readings from the relevant lore, or a communal activity.

V. *Conclusion.* The deities or spirits are thanked for their participation. There are closing prayers, and the participants are dismissed.

Building Blocks of Liturgy

Below are some key components of various liturgies.

Altars and Altar Maintenance

One must have a dedicated space to honor Thor, preferably in a location that is not disturbed by the mundane grind of quotidian life. Some people are fortunate to build a *vé* or *hof* on their property, but most of us construct simple shrines in our bedrooms or basements. In my own domicile, my wife and I have a bedroom set aside completely to our various shrines, and Thor's shrine sits atop a simple shelf.

Set up an altar with a candle, an offering bowl, and an incense burner with incense and some means to light it. A representation of Thor helps; statues of varying prices are readily available, but an image printed from the internet works. Red is Thor's color and many people decorate their altar with red fabric.

For rites, have a beverage handy—preferably of high-grade alcohol unless you cannot drink it yourself. Many Heathens use ritualistic drinking horns for their toasts. If you have a Thor's hammer for hallowing, place that on the altar as well. Finally, people who do runic divination often keep a set of runes and an omen journal on the altar.

After the ritual is over be sure to blow out any candles. Any food or liquid offerings should be disposed of outside in whatever manner best suits your circumstance and local laws.

A modern harrow (altar) to Thor and other Norse deities.
Photographed at Trothmoot 2018 by Ben Waggoner.

Invocation of Thor

It's best to create one's own prayer invoking the aspects of Thor that are most applicable to the rite, or are most congenial to the supplicants themselves. One can skim the Lore section in this work to reference episodes from Thor's exploits, and one can also use the poetic synonyms for Thor found in the Poetic Diction section.

The following is but an example:

"Thor, who bestrides the clouds on his goat-driven chariot. Descend from your hall of Bilskirnir. Thor, Slayer of Giants, warder of Midgard, be present at this rite and be welcome to this shrine."

One can also use poetry or song. An example of each has been included at the end of this chapter.

Statement of Purpose

Whether you are holding a solitary ritual or presiding over a small group, it's best to vocally state your intentions. That way, everyone—you, the deity concerned and any other participants—are cognizant of why you are bothering with the rite.

The statement could be as simple as: "I am here to honor Thor." It could be as complex as: "I, Jeremy, of the Baer family line, am here to honor Odin's eldest and greatest son, Thor. I give thanks to Red Beard and the Thunderer for the protection he has shown me and the prosperity with which he has blessed me. May I be considered a friend of Thor as I render these offerings willingly and gratefully. A gift for a gift."

Ritual Toast

A ritual toast is a short verbal honoring of a deity spoken just before imbibing a liquid offering. As an example: "Thor, I raise my glass (or mug or horn) to you, mighty son of Odin. May you protect me and grant me prosperity. [Drink]. Hail, Thor!" After said toast, pour the rest of the liquid, if there is any, into the offering bowl.

Offerings

Suggested offerings to Thor were fully discussed in the last chapter. In general, he seems to like strong drink, strong incense, and meat and cheese.

Prayer of Offering

When making a formal offering to the god, a short prayer should underscore the act. Example: "Thor, accept this offering. A gift for a gift."

Closing Prayer

One does not dismiss deities, much as one would not rudely eject an honored guest that had been invited. But one may give a polite signal that the rite is over and they may leave. As an example: "I have gifted Thor, and may he gift me in return. A gift for a gift. Thor, thank you for being at this rite. May your journey home to Thrudvang be filled with enjoyment. Hail Thor."

Runic Divination

There are various books on runic divination on the market for those unfamiliar.

When doing a divination to Thor, ask him what he wants. "Thor, be not silent and speak your will," or a similar prayer will suffice. Pull a rune or three, and preferably write it down in a journal kept specifically for such occasions. Spend some time meditating on it.

The Hammer Rite

The Hammer Rite is made by using one's hand or a hammer and tracing the form of a Thor's Hammer over the object or area one is hallowing. It's honestly a bit like making an upside-down cross: you make a long vertical stroke, then you make a shorter horizontal stroke between the mid-point and bottom. While doing this, one usually incants a short prayer. A common one is: "May Thor hallow and hold this holy stead."

It has been criticized by some that Heathens are aping Christians signing the Cross, or perhaps imitating ceremonial magick and its many ritualistic gestures such as the Lesser Banishing Ritual of the Pentagram (*Our Troth*, p. 454). In the Lore section, it was discussed that the saga of Hakon the Good contained an instance of the Hammer Rite that may or may not point to Heathen tradition. Regardless, I personally find that the Hammer Rite is both simple, effective and ultimately meaningful in the context of Heathenry.

The Two Powers

Magic is often seen as taking energy within oneself and redirecting it. Often, magic involves reconciling two seemingly opposite strands of energy into a third strand.

The Two Powers is one of the most widely used magical meditations in Druidry. The telluric energies of the earth below and the solar energies of the sky above are reconciled within the individual. This magical energy strengthens, empowers and protects (Wyndham, "Two Powers").

For this Thor Two Powers, I have used the healing and grounding powers of the earth, Thor's mother, as the telluric energies. The power of lightning from above, energizing and active, stands for the solar power.

Imagine yourself on top of a high mountain. Around you is a grove of oak trees. You stand in front of the highest oak tree: it seemingly touches the sky, and its branches are spread out widely in all directions, giving a sense of strength and welcoming hospitality.

Beneath you, the good green earth greets your feet. The earth is warm and inviting, the fields verdant and lush. Above you, the sunny sky begins to darken as rain clouds roll in. Thunder rumbles in the distance. The winds caress your face, a strong hint of forthcoming rain on them.

The rains begin, gently. The comfortable drizzle is refreshing, and the air smells pure and fresh. You breathe in the air while counting to four. Hold your breath for another four counts, then exhale slowly. Do this several times until your breath is rhythmic. Imagine the air purifying you and releasing your tensions as you proceed.

Once this is achieved, turn your attention downward to mother earth. You greet her formally with an intonation: "Hail Earth, mother of Thor!" Imagine tendrils of power extending from your inner being deep into the soils below. Visualize and feel the peaceful energies of the earth ride the tendrils upward until they merge with your own energies. You may wish to inhale deeply, drawing these energies into yourself as you do. Imagine these energies healing and nurturing your being. You affirm the powers formally, "Hail Earth, mother of Thor. I am fed and sustained by these powers!"

Now turn your attention upward. The sky has been completely overtaken by dark clouds, pregnant with rain and lightning. Thunder crashes all around you. "Hail Thor, Thunderer!" you exclaim. Imagine tendrils of power extending from your inner being into the storm clouds above. As you inhale you draw into yourself the electric energies of the lightning above. The lightning is among the greatest energies of the cosmos; it invigorates, it strengthens, it empowers. Once you have fed on these energies to your satisfaction, acknowledge Thor thusly: "Hail, Thor, I am strengthened by your lightning."

With this being done, split your attention between the earth and sky. Take the energies of the earth and the sky into yourself simultaneously. Feel these two powers mixing, forming a combined energy in the process. This energy sweeps through your entire being. It heals and nurtures, it strengthens and sustains. Acknowledge this feeling: "I stand between earth and sky, between Mother Earth and the Thunderer. I take these powers within me. I am nurtured and empowered by them."

When you have done this to your satisfaction, you can then gently bring your attention back to the outer world and end the meditation. The meditation exists on two fronts: for its own sake as a general grounding and centering tool, or as a prelude to work further magic. If one is new to the Two Powers, one should probably practice it daily for a week or three before one tries anything else with it.

Protection Rite

The Protection Rite can be used on its own, but works especially well as a follow-up from a Two Powers meditation.

Visualize and feel yourself brimming with protective and nurturing energies. You will now need to direct those energies with either your fingers, or else a special tool that has been ritually consecrated for magical purposes.

Trace the sign of the hammer in front of you. As you go visualize a large, thick energy barrier that can repel harm and ill-will. In counter-clockwise formation turn 90 degrees and do the same thing. Keep doing this until you have completed a circle. Now do this above and below. When that is done, return to your starting position and concentrate. Feel and visualize all six points around you—front, rear, right, left, above, and below—as guarded by an etheric barrier.

Say a prayer of affirmation along these lines: "Hammer in front, Hammer behind. Hammer to my right and left. Hammer above and below. By the might of Thor I am protected from harm. Hail Thor!"

Daily Rituals

Now that we have studied the flow of liturgy and the building blocks of liturgy, it's time to perform liturgy. I have included rituals that are largely devotional but incorporate a magical aspect as well.

Heathen Solitary Ritual

This is a simple ritual, designed to build a devotional relation to Thor through an offering, toast, and runic divination.

I. Introduction
       A: Pre-ritual set-up of Altar
       B: Hallowing (Hammer Rite)
       C: Statement of Purpose
II. Rising Action
       A. Tending to the Altar (light candles, incense, etc.)
       B. Invocation of Thor
III. Climax
       A. Offering
       B. Prayer of Offering
IV. Falling Action
       A. Runic Divination
       B. Ritual Toast to Thor

V. Conclusion
    A. Closing Prayer
    B. Tending to the Altar (blow out candles, etc.).

With some imagination and a few modifications, this ritual can be adapted to small groups. The officiant simply changes any statements from "I" to "we" and "my" to "our" where appropriate. Instead of an altar, one might have a bonfire or campfire as a focus point. For the ritual toast, the horn/cup/mug is passed around the participants and each individual has a chance to quickly hail Thor.

Druidic Ritual
    This Druid ritual involves a devotional aspect through its offering, but also focuses on Thor as a figure of nature reverence and natural energies.

I. Introduction
    A: Pre-ritual set up
    B: Purification using mugwort or juniper
    C: Statement of Purpose
II. Rising Action
    A. Tending to the Altar
    B. Invocation of Thor
III. Climax
    A. Offering
    B. Prayer of Offering
IV. Falling Action
    A: Two Powers Meditation
V. Conclusion
    A. Closing Prayer
    B. Tending to the Altar

The outline is very close to the Heathen ritual already discussed, except for the following changes:

The *hallowing* section using the Hammer Rite, a distinctly Heathen practice, is replaced with more generic *purification* by smudging the area with appropriate incense. Mugwort is well within the Germanic tradition; juniper is more Celtic but works within this Druidic framework. White sage is widely used by pagans, but has come under fire recently, owing to environmental concerns and perceptions of cultural appropriation from Native Americans.

The Two Powers as a magical meditation is used as the esoteric focal point, replacing the runic divination.

One's invocations to Thor would probably do well to emphasize his progeny from the earth, and his role as giver of fertility and the rains. This places it within the spirit of nature reverence that is a hallmark of most Druidic systems.

This can be adapted to small group practice provided the officiant is qualified to lead a guided meditation of The Two Powers.

Occult Ritual for Protection

The following ritual opens with a Heathen Hammer rite, incorporates the Two Powers meditation of the Druidic rite, and adds a magical ritual for some basic occult protection.

I. Introduction
    A: Pre-ritual set-up
    B: Hallowing (Hammer Rite)
    C: Statement of Purpose
II. Rising Action
    A. Tending to the Altar
    B. Invocation of Thor
III. Climax
    A. Offering
    B. Prayer of Offering
IV. Falling Action
    A: Two Powers
    B: Protection Rite
    C: (optional) Runic Divination
V. Conclusion
    A. Closing Prayer
    B. Tending to the Altar

Consecration of Hammer

While one can, in a pinch, consecrate space with one's fingers, in the long term it is best to buy or make ritual tools to that effect. The obvious choice of tools in working with Thor would be a hammer. (A small sledge-hammer with a wooden handle, from your local hardware store, will do nicely if you can't make or buy a custom one; the handle can be decorated by wood-burning or painting as desired.) The hammer (or whatever tool) should then be consecrated. The following is a suggested outline for such.

    I. Introduction
           A: Pre-ritual set-up of Altar
           B: Hallowing (Hammer Rite)
           C: Statement of Purpose
    II. Rising Action
           A. Tending to the Altar
           B. Invocation of Thor
    III. Climax
           A. Offering
           B. Prayer of Offering
    IV. Falling Action
           A. Consecration of Tool
    V. Conclusion
           A. Closing Prayer
           B. Tending to the Altar

Hallowing

Presumably you have been making the sign of the hammer with your fingers up to this point. This will be the last time you use your fingers, for this rite presumes you have bought or forged a hammer (or some other tool) and will be consecrating it in due course.

Statement of Purpose

"Hail Thor, hallowing god, you who keep the forces of chaos at bay. I/ we have come to consecrate this hammer/tool to you, that I/we may wield it in your name to forge sacred space."

Invocation of Thor

"Thor, warder of Midgard, you who hallow by fire and by lightning. May you be present at this rite. As you are the god who guards against chaos. I/we invite you hither. Hail Thor."

Prayer of Offering

"Thor, I give this gift to you that you may give back to me. A gift for a gift. Hail Thor!"

Consecration of Tool

There are a variety of things that could be done here.

First, if you feel so inclined, I'd recommend purifying the ritual object by lighting mugwort or juniper incense, then passing the object through the smoke a few times.

Next, you could, if you so wish, perform the Two Powers Meditation while clutching the object.

Finally, and most importantly, is a prayer of consecration. I would recommend visualizing Thor striking the object with lightning while intoning something along these lines: "Thor, strongest of the gods and wielder of Mjolnir. May you imbue this object with your might and main. I consecrate this hammer/tool to you that it may ward away chaos and evil. I consecrate this hammer/tool to you that it may forge sacred space. Hail Thor."

Holidays and Holiday Rituals

The Scandinavian sources mention three or four Heathen holidays. *Yule* was more of a season than a holiday, and obviously the most important holiday which later was co-opted by the church as Christmas. *Winter Nights* is mentioned as a harvest sacrifice around mid-October, when reverence was especially paid to ancestral and local spirits; it was not unlike the Celtic Samhain. A *dísablót* honoring female ancestors (*dísir*) seems to have taken place sometime in February. Finally, in the spring, there was a *sigrblót*, or victory blót, to Odin for a successful military campaigning season.

None of these holidays specifically reference Thor.

Many modern Heathen groups will incorporate the first two or three holidays mentioned, and then throw in their own. Some groups try to follow an eight-fold "Wheel of the Year" which is popular in Wicca and general Neopaganism; others follow their own schedules.

Below are some ideas to honor Thor at holy days.

Thorrablót

Some individuals and groups observe a *Thorrablót* (*Þórrablót*). The holiday in question seems to be dedicated to a legendary king Thorri, rather than the god Thor (*Our Troth*, p. 358). The origins of this holiday are disputed: while it's indisputably a winter festival, it may not have been particularly pagan. In any case, it fell into abeyance in the Medieval era. It was resurrected by Icelandic students in 1873, and became widespread in Iceland in the post-World War II era (Valgardsson, "Iceland's Ugly Food Festival"). The idea is that by winter's end, food supplies are low and people resort to the hardiest stuff that is left over. The array of culinarily dubious items includes fermented shark, or *hákarl* (Valgardsson, "Iceland's Ugly Food Festival"). In recent times, a special beer made from whale testicles is imbibed during this holiday (Lockheart, "Icelandic Craft Beer").

Regardless of the origins of this holiday, some have elected to honor Thor in late January (with or without disgusting food and drink) and give thanks for getting through the winter (*Our Troth*, pp. 360-361).

Below I present an outline of a suggested *Thorrablót* ritual.

I. Introduction
    A: Pre-ritual set-up of Altar
    B: Hallowing (Hammer Rite)
    C: Statement of Purpose
II. Rising Action
    A. Tending to the Altar
    B. Invocation of Thor
III. Climax
    A. Offering
    B. Prayer of Offering
IV. Falling Action
    A. Runic Divination
    B. Ritual Toast to Thor
V. Conclusion
    A. Closing Prayer
    B. Tending to the Altar

Statement of Purpose:

"I/we are here to honor Thor, as protector of man and giver of fertility. I/we give thanks to Thor for the gifts he furnishes: fertile fields and protection. May Thor see us safely through the end of winter."

Invocation to Thor:

"Thor, enemy of the frost giants, you who ensure the fecundity of the fields. Be here now. I/we call to you to honor you and to ask your blessings on this late winter's day."

Prayer of Offering:

"Thor, I/we give this offering to you that you may in turn give back to me/us. I/we thank you for the food we eat, and I/we ask that you may provide for us till winter's end. Thor, accept this offering!"

Loafmass

Bread was vitally important to the Anglo-Saxons, not only as a source of sustenance, but as a communal activity that brought people together (Pollington, *The Meadhall*, p. 37). Its importance is symbolized by the fact that the Anglo-Saxon word for lord translates as "loaf keeper" (Pollington, *The Meadhall*, p. 184).

There was an Anglo-Saxon holiday known as *Hlaf-mas*, which is sometimes Celticized as *Lammas* or rendered in modern English as *Loafmass*. It commemorates the wheat harvest (BBC, "Lughnasadh"). Some groups, especially in the Anglo-Saxon sphere, honor Thor/Thunor in his agricultural aspects on this holiday. I was once an active member of Great Valley Kindred, an Anglo-Saxon group, where we dedicated this holiday to him (Great Valley Kindred "Our Holidays").

Below I present an outline of a suggested Loafmass rite, done Anglo-Saxon style. We'll be replacing "Thor" with "Thunor," and we will also be using a different form of hallowing. The date of the first wheat harvest varies by local circumstance; however, in the Northern Hemisphere, many polytheists influenced by the Neopagan "Wheel of the Year" typically celebrate it somewhere around August 1.

I. Introduction
    A: Pre-ritual set-up of Altar
    B: Hallowing (fire around the *weofod*)
    C: Statement of Purpose
II. Rising Action
    A. Tending to the Altar
    B. Invocation of Thunor
III. Climax
    A. Offering
    B. Prayer of Offering
IV. Falling Action
    A. Runic Divination
    B. Ritual Toast to Thunor
V. Conclusion
    A. Closing Prayer
    B. Tending to the Altar

Hallowing:

In Old English, *wih* means sacred (Pollington, *The Elder Gods*, p. 143). From this word comes *weoh*, or sacred idol, and thus *weofod*, or altar.

Instead of the Hammer Rite, many Anglo-Saxon groups hallow by circumambulating around the *weofod* with fire. This is easily enough done in public rites where a campfire or bonfire is a focal point. In a solitary rite in one's home, if the *weofod* is backed up against a corner or wall, circumambulating might not be practical. Instead one could simply stand in front of the altar with a consecrated flame.

In any case, one should implore Thunor in the act with a short prayer. "Thunor, make sacred this space," or "Thunor, hallow with this flame," would work well enough.

Statement of Purpose:

"I/we are here to give thanks to Thunor for the first harvest. The fields are ripe with grain, ready to give over their bounty. I/we honor Thunor, god of the fields and the farmers."

Invocation of Thunor:

"Thunor, son of Woden, you who hallow by flame and lightning. I/we invite you hither. I/we gave thanks for the harvest and the fertile fields of wheat. Be here now, and attend my/our rite. Hail Thunor!"

Prayer of Offering

"Thunor, for the fruits of the first harvest, I/we give thanks. A gift for a gift. Thunor, accept this offering!"

For this particular holiday, a bread baked by oneself for the holiday would be an especially suitable offering.

Closing Prayer

"Thunor, for your gifts, I/we have given you gifts in return. I/we thank you for attending my/our rite. May you now depart, but remember us with good will. Hail Thunor!"

First Thunderstorm

I once lived on the edge of the Appalachian Mountains. Pennsylvania, Maryland and West Virginia ostensibly have sharp boundaries on a political map, but in this particular area the three states grade into each other seamlessly through the landscape of sylvan hills and rolling streams.

The seasons could vary somewhat from year to year, but generally the snows melted in late March or early April—not long after the vernal equinox. With spring came the first thunderstorms of the year. I made a point to honor Thor when the first thunderstorm came, greeting his arrival and hailing the retreat of the proverbial frost giants.

There is no lore to this, and I am not aware of other groups doing anything along this line. But it was meaningful to me, and seemed like a condign way to honor Thor. When the spring air hits the Appalachians, the world seemingly comes to life. And when the air rumbles with thunder, saturated with electric fire, you can feel the presence of a god.

How groups or individuals adapt their liturgy to their own local circumstance is a fascinating tale which I think deserves its own book. But I would suggest that to have a modern spiritual faith, as opposed to some museum textbook recreation, people can and should find different ways to bring Thor into their own circumstances. May you find what works for you.

Below is a suggested outline (druidic style) of how to honor Thor for the first thunderstorm.

I. Introduction
    A: Pre-ritual set up
    B: Purification using mugwort or juniper
    C: Statement of Purpose
II. Rising Action
    A. Tending to the Altar
    B. Invocation of Thor
III. Climax
    A. Offering
    B. Prayer of Offering
IV. Falling Action
    A: Two Powers Meditation
    B: Runic Divination
V. Conclusion
    A. Closing Prayer
    B. Tending to the Altar

Statement of Purpose
"I/we have come to honor Thor for the first thunderstorm. Spring brings with it the first rains, and the first lightning. As Mother Earth teems with life, let me/us honor Thor."

Invocation of Thor

"Thor, son of earth, may you be here now at this rite. Protector of man, warder of the fields, hail to you. As dark storm clouds gather above, as the air explodes with fury, I/we honor you. Hail!"

Prayer of Offering

"Thor, Thunderer from above. You who drive your goat-driven chariot through the heavens. Thor, you who keep the frost giants at bay. May you bless the fields with life-giving rain. Thor, may you accept this offering!"

Two Powers Meditation

The Two Powers as described earlier in this chapter needs no revision, but the first thunderstorm of the year is an especially powerful time to perform it.

Closing Prayer

"Thor, son of earth, you who thunder above. I/we have gifted you for the first thunder, Whenever the skies crackle above with your fury, may I/we remember you. Hail Thor!"

Poetry

Odin is the god of skalds, but we saw in the historical age that there were poets who composed verses to Thor. Skaldic poetry is a matter of taste but many moderns, myself included, find that any spiritual reverence becomes lost in its complicated style. Poetry, regardless of its form, is nonetheless a suitable offering to Thor. The god provided a beached whale to a starving Thorhall in exchange for a poem.

The following is a quick poem I have used for liturgy as an invocation to Thor, which he seems to like. Feel free to use it if you like.

> *Thor,*
> *you are the storm that rages day and night.*
> *You are the cloud that conceals sun from sight.*
> *You are the wind that thrashes in its throes.*
> *You are the bolt that harrows all its foes.*
> *You are the fury of tempests well-wrought.*
> *You are the power of battles hard fought.*

You are the warder who dispels ill-wights.
You are the hammer that upholds all rites.
Hail Thor!

Song to Thor
written by Laura "Snow" Fuller

According to Tacitus, the ancient tribes sang battle songs to the Germanic "Hercules." In a UPG session, Thor indicated he wanted more songs sung to him in this modern age, to gather his followers around in fellowship. This may also be used as an invocation in a solitary rite.

Hail Thor, Friend of Man.
You who guard and love the land.
Raise your hammer, slay your foes.
And feed their eyes to Odin's crows.

Friends and Family here.
Raise your horn of mead or beer.
Sing a song and drink your fill.
Gather here all you of good will.

Skalds tell stories of the past,
Of swinging swords and horses fast.
When shield maidens fought back to back.
Bright lightning strikes and thunders crack!

Hail Thor, Friend of Man.
You who guard and love the land.
Lend your strength to friends gathered here.
Round the fire, with those of good cheer.

Child of Earth and Odin's son
In the eve when battles are won
Gather us into your hall,
That we may answer friendship's call.

Thor and his wife Sif.
Smythe, *A Primary Reader* (1896)

Chapter Thirteen: A Woman's Perspective

by Laura "Snow" Fuller

I have been asked, on more than one occasion, how I, as a feminist, work with the most manly of Gods. After all, while Odin and Loki are well documented for their gender-bending escapades, Thor is less than thrilled to put on a wedding dress, even for the critical mission of retrieving his hammer.

Thor, the strongest of Gods, the wielder of the mighty Mjolnir, the husband of Sif, seems to embody what even today we see as a masculine ideal. He is stronger than anyone else, he is a protector, a hallower. He's a good father and husband, defending his wife's honor when it is called into question. In a word, he is everything that is pushed into the stereotype of a cis-het-male that so often feminists consider toxic to healthy relationships.

I certainly cannot answer for *everyone*. Everyone has different experiences. What I share with you is my own personal experience and UPG on the matter. If it helps you, great. If not, feel free to move along.

I first met Thor when I was a teenager. I was going through a phase where I was questioning religion in general and Christianity in particular. I was feeling disconnected from Christianity because I did not feel it represented women fairly. Women weren't able to be priests, and the ones who were sainted were those who were meekly obedient. Growing up, I had not met my biological father. My parents were not married and he was completely absent from my life. He didn't support us financially and I had never even seen his picture. While historically, this isn't an unusual family structure, at the time it WAS unusual for middle class white families. Some of my friends had divorced parents, but they did all KNOW both their parents. I felt like I was completely different, and Christianity did not have a model for our family structure. Especially not in the Catholic Church.

Anyway, I was rebelling. Our high school choir was on tour and we were singing in quite a few churches. One of the churches we were to sing during their church service. I didn't want to participate, especially when they told me I was to wear their church robe and a heavy crucifix necklace. I asked to be excused from the performance, but our director said if I didn't sing, he'd give me a failing grade for the day. So, I donned the robe and necklace feeling awful.

As I did, I heard this deep voice saying to me not to worry about it, he'd fix it for me. At the time, I had no idea who it was and thought I was hearing things. As we were processing into the sanctuary, I was literally poised one foot about to step over the threshold when, out of a clear sky, a bolt of lightning hit the steeple of the church. All the power went out. The organ stopped mid-note. Fuses blew. Mass was cancelled.

It was glorious.

From that moment on, I knew that there was someone watching out for me. Someone had my back. I didn't know who, but I knew it to the core of my being. I didn't figure out who it was until twenty or so years later when I discovered Ásatrú.

In my practice today, I work primarily with four deities: Odin, Freya, Skadi, and Thor. The more time I spend working with Thor, and the deeper my practice grows, the more the idea of a feminist avoiding him seems silly. Many characterizations of feminists are the very things that Thor encourages in his followers:

- Strength, both internal and physical.
- Self-reliance.
- Hard work.
- Taking a stand for what's right.
- Protecting the weak.
- Defending justice and order and society.

Throughout the Lore, Thor smashes anything that threatens the Æsir. He is the defender of the folk, of the *innangard*, of the farmland and fields that sustain society.

Some might argue that feminists focus their rhetoric in one of two ways, either as liberal or as radical. Liberal feminists want a bigger piece of the pie. Radical feminists say the pie is rotten, they want to bake a new pie. On the surface, this seems to be the opposite of what Thor stands for: protecting the created order of the cosmos. But when we consider why feminists say the order is misaligned, we see the role Thor can play in a feminist Heathenry.

Feminism is about equality, about not judging people based on their sex or their gender identity. Feminism is about allowing people, all people, to have choices. Choose to work or stay home with your family. Choose to have a family or not. To get married or not. To express yourself as your true self, so long as that expression doesn't cause harm. Embracing this mindset is where inner strength begins, and that is where Thor enters the picture.

Thor encourages the strength to stand up for what's right for you and for those important to you. To defend the weak. While "Social Justice Warrior" is seen by some as a pejorative term, the idea that one should stop at nothing to make the world a better place aligns very closely with my experiences with Thor.

If you seek to find your inner strength, to push yourself for the betterment of your society, then Thor is one who can and will help you. And if you are willing to share a beer (good, strong, dark beer), or a coffee, or some meat and cheese with him while you chat, so much the better.

Thor with his Hammer.
Smythe, *A Primary Reader* (1896)

Summary of Modern Experience

Thor can offer many things to many different peoples and groups. To modern Heathens he can be essentially what he was to historical Heathens: protector of man, giver of fertility, champion of Heathen tradition. To Druids and other earth-centric Neopagans, Thor, son of the earth and wielder of lightning, offers a powerful figure upon whom to meditate. To occultists of various stripes, Thor may lend his energies for hallowing and protection.

Regardless of how we view him, we approach him through the means of liturgy. Rituals can have a definite structure and purpose and yet still be simple and direct enough to be easily performed as a solitary or in a small group. Rituals can serve both votive and magical ends. Through prayers, poetry and song we celebrate the majesty of Thor. Holidays, whether invented or loosely based on historic precedent, can be set aside to honor Odin's son.

It is my feeling that Thor is largely an affable deity, blessed with practical intelligence, who wants the best for his followers. He does make a few demands, of course, as gods are wont to do. It is my hope that followers of Thor can share details about how they perceive the Thunderer, about what he desires and promises. When enough of these expressions of personal gnosis are shared, commonalities can be discerned, and perhaps a workable *cultus* can be achieved.

Finally, I have presented Thor from my own experience. The concluding essay, however, written by my wife, attests to the fact that any gender can have meaningful and empowering experiences with this god.

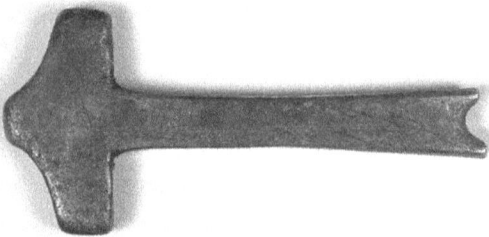

Silver Thor's Hammer amulet, with a broken suspension hole at the end of the handle. Portable Antiquities Scheme, British Museum, LANCUM-ED9222. CC BY-SA 4.0.

Afterword

In writing the first two sections of this work, I learned one or two new things myself. In writing the third section, I was forced to refine existing yet unfiltered personal thoughts. In so many words, writing this work has been not only a devotional exercise, but a learning experience of my own. That is honestly the best type of endeavor: when our hearts and heads are aligned to the same holy purpose, and our fingers gleefully do the work, demanding though it may be.

It is my hope that this work adds a considered voice to modern Heathenry and paganism. Gods can sometimes be like people in a group: the flashy ones get all the attention (Odin), the infamous ones get all the notoriety (Loki), but the straight-laced ones simply doing their jobs don't always get the recognition they deserve. Hopefully this work helps elevate Thor's arguably undervalued and overlooked status.

As I finish writing this work in March of 2019, the world is torn yet again by acts of religious violence and bigotry. The world can be a weary place; sometimes hiding in a cave seems preferable to dealing with its nonsense. And yet live in the world we must.

I hope my words inspire to bring people together rather than tear them apart. Thor is a god for the masses, not the elite, and I firmly believe he would see people of good heart and cheer enjoined in fellowship to protect their communities. Historical Heathens saw Thor as defending Midgard from the forces of chaos; in the twilight of their religion Heathens saw Thor as the champion of their tradition against the Christians who sought their conversion. It's my hope that in this modern age Thor, and his followers, help save Heathenry from the miscreants who would use the gods as ciphers of their politically motivated bigotry and violence.

Works Cited

BBC. "Lughnasadh." 06 July 2011. Web. 18 March 2019. <http://www.bbc.co.uk/religion/religions/paganism/holydays/lughnasadh.shtml>.

Blair, Peter Hunter. *An Introduction to Anglo-Saxon England.* 3rd Edition. Cambridge: Cambridge University Press, 2003. Print.

Bonewits, Isaac. *Neopagan Rites: A Guide to Creating Rituals That Work.* Woodbury: Llewellyn Publications, 2007. Print.

Branston, Brian. *The Lost Gods of England.* London: Constable and Company, 1993. Print.

Byock, Jesse L. *Viking Age Iceland.* New York: Penguin Books, 2001. Print.

Caesar, Julius; H. J. Edwards, trans. *The Gallic War.* Cambridge, Mass.: Harvard University Press, 1917. Print.

Carr-Gomm, Phillip. "A Longer History of Druidry." 2006. Web. 18th March 2019. <https://www.druidry.org/druid-way/what-druidry/brief-history-druidry/longer-history-druidry>.

Davidson, H. R. Ellis. *Gods and Myths of Northern Europe.* New York: Penguin Books, 1990. Print.

Driscoll, Matthew James. "A New Edition of the *Fornaldarsögur Norðurlanda*: Some Basic Questions." *On Editing Old Scandinavian Texts: Problems and Perspectives.* M. Bampi and F. Ferrari, eds. Trento: Universitá da Trento, 2009. pp. 71-84. Web. 28th February 2019. <http://www.driscoll.dk/docs/driscoll-new_edition.pdf>.

Editors of Encyclopedia Brittanica. *Swastika.* n.d. Web. 6th March 2019. <https://www.britannica.com/topic/swastika>.

Enright, Michael J. *Lady With a Mead Cup: Ritual, Prophecy and Lorship in the European Warband from La Tene to the Viking Age.* Portland: Fair Courts Press, 2013. Print.

"Eulogy on Thor." n.d. *The World Tree Project.* Web. 4 March 2019. <http://www.worldtreeproject.org/document/2288>.

Faulkner, Dr. Neil. "Overview: Roman Britain." 29 March 2011. Web. 5 March 2019. <http://www.bbc.co.uk/history/ancient/romans/overview_roman_01.shtml>.

Ferguson, Robert. *The Vikings: A History*. New York: Penguin Books, 2010. Print.

Flowers, Stephen. *The Galdrabók: An Icelandic Grimoire*. York Beach: Samuel Weiser, Inc., 1989. Print.

Great Valley Kindred. "Our Holidays." n.d. Web. 4th March 2019. <https://greatvalleykindred.com/events/our-holidays/>.

Grønle, Sian, trans. "Kristni Saga." *Islendingabok and Kristni Saga*. London: University College London, 2006. Print.

Haywood, John. *The Penguin Historical Atlas of the Vikings*. New York: Penguin, 1995. Print.

Heather, Peter. *Empire and Barbarians: The Fall of Rome and the Birth of Europe*. New York: Oxford University Press, 2009. Print.

Hollander, Lee M., trans. *The Poetic Edda*. Austin: University of Texas Press, Austin, 2011. Print.

Iovi Optimo Maximo: to Jupiter Best and Greatest. n.d. Web. 24 March 2019. <http://www.deomercurio.be/en/iom.html>.

Joe, Jimmy. "Teutonic Deities." 10/10/2000. Web. 5th March 2019. <http://www.timelessmyths.com/norse/teutonic.html#Donar>.

Johnson, Ben. "Timeline of Roman Britain." n.d. Web. 5th March 2019. <https://www.historic-uk.com/HistoryUK/HistoryofBritain/Timeline-of-Roman-Britain/>.

Kellog, Robert. "Introduction." *The Sagas of the Icelanders*. Ed. Ornolfur Thorsson. New York, New York: Penguin Books, 2001. Print.

Kunz, Keneva, trans. "Eirik The Red's Saga." *The Sagas of Icelanders*. New York: Penguin, 2000. Print.

Larrington, Carolyne, trans. *The Poetic Edda*. New York: Oxford University Press, 2008. Print.

Lockheart, Katie. "This Icelandic Craft Beer is Made from a Giant Whale Testicle.' 11 August 2018. Web. 4th March 2019. < https://www.yahoo.com/lifestyle/icelandic-craft-beer-made-giant-120001337.html>

Macleod, Mindy and Mees, Bernard. *Runic Amulets and Magic Objects*. Woodbridge: The Boydell Press, 2006. Print.

Mallory, J.P. *In Search of the Indo-Europeans: Language, Archaeology and Myth*. New York: Thames and Hudson, 1989. Print.

Mark, Joshua J. "Vortigern." 23 May 2017. Web. 5th March 2019. <https://www.ancient.eu/Vortigern/>.

McKinnel, John and Rudolf Simek. *Runes, Magic and Religion*. Vienna: Verlag Fassbender, 2004. Print.

"Of Oaks and Axes." 5 June 2018. Web. 5th March 2019. <https://www.catholictextbookproject.com/this-week-in-history-blogposts/of-oaks-and-axes/>.

"Old Saxon Baptismal Vow." n.d. 5 March 2019. <http://self.gutenberg.org/articles/eng/old_saxon_baptismal_vow>.

Palsson, Hermann and Paul Edwards, trans. *Gautrek's Saga and Other Medieval Tales*. New York: New York University Press, 1968. Print.

—. *Eyrbyggja Saga*. New York: Penguin Books, 1989. Print.

Pollington, Stephen. *Runes: Literacy in the Germanic Iron Age*. Anglo-Saxon Books, 2016. Print.

—. *The Elder Gods: The Otherworld of Early England*. Anglo-Saxon Books, 2011. Print.

—. *The Meadhall*. Anglo-Saxon Books, 2010. Print.

Ray, Rebecca. "The Five Act Play (Dramatic Structure)." n.d. Web. 18 March 2019. <https://www.storyboardthat.com/articles/e/five-act-structure>.

Saxo Grammaticus; Peter Fisher, trans. *The History of the Danes, Books I-IX*. Cambridge: D. S. Brewer, 1996. Print.

Schreiwer, Robert L. *The First Book of Urglaawe Myths*. Bristol, Penn.: Deitscherei.com, 2014. Print.

Schreiwer, Robert and Ammerili Eckhart. *A Dictionary of Urglaawe Terminology*. Bristol: www.urglaawe.org, 2012. Print.

Serith, Ceisiwr. "Proto-Indo-European Deities." n.d. Web. 4th March 2019. <http://www.ceisiwrserith.com/pier/deities.htm>.

—. "What Was Proto-Indo-European Religion Like?" n.d. Web. 4th March 2019. <http://www.ceisiwrserith.com/pier/whatwasreligion.htm>.

Snorri Sturluson; Erling Momsen and A. H. Smith, trans. *Heimskringla, or The Lives of the Norse Kings*. New York: Dover Publications, 1990. Print.

—. *The Prose Edda*. Trans. Jesse L Byock. New York: Penguin Books, 2005. Print.

Tacitus, Cornelius; M. Hutton and E. H. Warmington, trans. *Dialogus, Agricola, Germania*. Loeb Classical Library. Cambridge, Mass.: Harvard University Press, 1980. Print.

The Troth. *Our Troth. Volume I: History and Lore*. Ed. Kveldulf Hagan Gundarsson.. 2nd ed. North Charleston : BookSurge, LLC, 2006. Print.

—. *Our Troth*. Ed. Kveldulf Gundarsson. 2nd ed. North Charleston: BookSurge Publishing, 2007. Print.

Thomas, Rev. Kirk. "The Nature of Sacrifice." 1 March 2008. Web. 4th

March 2019. <https://www.adf.org/articles/cosmology/nature-of-sacrifice.html>.

Todd, Malcolm. *The Early Germans*. Malden: Blackwell Publishers, 1992. Print.

Tolley, Clive. *Shamanism in Norse Myth and Magic*. Vol. 1. Helsinki: Academia Scientiarum Fennica, 2009. Print.

Turville-Petre, E. O. G. *Myth and Religion of the North: Religion of Ancient Scandinavia*. Westport: Greenwood Press, 1975. Print.

Valgardsson, E. Marie. "Iceland's Ugly Food Festival (Thorrablot) Is Here." 17 February 2015. *Icelandic Times*. Web. 4th March 2019. <https://icelandictimes.com/icelands-ugly-food-festival-thorrablot-is-here/>.

Waggoner, Ben, trans. "Gautrek's Saga." *Six Sagas of Adventure*. New Haven, Conn.: The Troth, 2014.

Wyndham, Jeffrey Rev. "Two Powers." 05 November 2010. Web. 18 March 2019. <https://www.adf.org/rituals/meditations/two-powers.html>.

Illustrations:

Bray, Olive (W. G. Collingwood, illust.) *The Elder or Poetic Edda, Commonly Known as Saemund's Edda. Part I—The Mythological Poems*. London: The Viking Club, 1908.

Brown, Abbie Farwell (E. Boyd Smith, illust.) *In the Days of Giants: A Book of Norse Tales*. Boston: Houghton Mifflin, 1902.

Guerber, H. A. *Myths of the Norsemen from the Eddas and Sagas*. London: George G. Harrap, 1919.

Keary, A. and E. Keary. *The Heroes of Asgard: Tales from Scandinavian Mythology*. London: MacMillan, 1871.

Smythe, E. Louise. *A Primary Reader: Old-Time Stories, Fairy Tales & Myths*. Chicago: Werner School Book Company, 1895.

Stephens, George. *Thunor the Thunderer, Carved on a Scandinavian Font of About the Year 1000*. London: Williams and Norgate, 1878.

Stephens, George. *Professor S. Bugge's Studies on Northern Mythology Shortly Examined*. London: Williams and Norgate, 1883.

Thorsen, Peder Goth. *De Danske Runemindesmærker*. Copenhagen: Hagerup, 1879.

Wagner, Richard (Margaret Armour, transl.; Arthur Rackham, illust.) *The Rhinegold and The Valkyrie*. London: William Heinemann 1910.